Come On In

taking the
hassle out
of hospitality

Lisa Bogart

Be my guest Marilyn!
LOVE Lisa 2001

BEACON HILL PRESS
OF KANSAS CITY

ISBN-13: 978-0-8341-2311-3
ISBN-10: 0-8341-2311-8

Printed in the
United States of America

Cover Design: Chad A. Cherry
Interior Design: Sharon Page

Library of Congress Cataloging-in-Publication Data

Bogart, Lisa, 1960-
    Come on in : taking the hassle out of hospitality / Lisa Bogart.
        p. cm.
    Includes bibliographical references and index.
    ISBN-13: 978-0-8341-2311-3 (pbk.)
    ISBN-10: 0-8341-2311-8 (pbk.)
    1. Hospitality—Religious aspects—Christianity. I. Title.

    BV4647.H67B64 2007
    241'.671—dc22

                                                    2007000417

10 9 8 7 6 5 4 3 2 1

Contents

Introduction   5

1. Cleaning the House and Your Heart   7

2. Excuses, Excuses   35

3. Come On In   43

4. Let's Party   75

5. The Littlest Hostess   103

6. Grandma Know-How   121

7. Beyond Your Backyard   139

8. Thanks for Coming   163

Recipes Index   185

Web Sites and Other Resources   187

Introduction

I love to throw a party! I design the invitations, plan the party favors, and go wild in the kitchen. Every now and then I yearn for a talent that involves more flash—musical performance maybe, or public speaking. But what I'm good at is creating a special moment. And I cherish my gift; it's a way for me to express God's love.

I like to put out my china and crystal, buy flowers, and make party favors. But I realize not everyone feels as comfortable with entertaining as I do. I'm here to tell you that hospitality comes with many different shapes, sizes, and price tags. One is just right for you.

If you want to create an environment where people feel comfortable and cared for, you have everything it takes to be hospitable. The rest is only tricks of the trade.

I'm going to share with you some ideas that will enhance your current comfort level with hospitality. Whether you're very reluctant to have friends over or would just like some new ideas for entertaining, you'll enjoy what follows. We'll look at several ways to entertain: simple, low-key, and spontaneous; something that takes a little more effort to create; and sumptuous entertaining when you can plan ahead and want to be extravagant.

God has a world to redeem, and He uses every method available from worldwide evangelism to neighborhood get-togethers. Hospitality started with the graciousness of God's heart, so we'll start with *your* heart.

Put aside anxiety, relax, and come on in. . . .

1

Cleaning the House and Your Heart

Hospitality is about more than a clean house and gourmet food. It's really about building relationships. In a perfect world, we will welcome drop-in visitors and find an uncluttered place for them to sit. And for invited guests, we will do a little planning ahead—drag out the vacuum, clean the bathroom, and think about what we'll serve our guests.

There is, however, something much more important than cooking and cleaning. What is essential in building relationships through hospitality is the condition of your heart and attitude. Hostessing may come naturally to you, or maybe you feel you need some help in developing your hospitality skills. Either way, God asks us all to welcome guests to our table. Do we do as He asks with joy or with a sense of obligation? All of us have our own unique ways of sharing this gift. So let's look beyond the snack table and see what's available at the main buffet.

God sets a feast table of blessings before you, and He pours grace into your life. Hospitality is a gift He wants you to open. He wants you to smile with pleasure and say, "Thank you, I can hardly wait to use my gift. It's going to be so much fun!" He knows it is just perfect for you.

Does hospitality fit you as if it were tailor-made the first time you try it on? Or is it a little tight in the shoulders? Is it a fun thing you want to use right away, or are you ready to return it? As God has showered you with His love and graciousness, He wants you to mirror His love and graciousness to His world—using your gift of hospitality.

To prepare your heart and attitude for this gift, this first chapter is a collection of devotionals that will help you see the spiritual value of serving others through hospitality. Reflect on these thoughts and think about ways you can love others.

The Menu Varies

Do you love eating out? There are so many restaurants I enjoy. The Cheesecake Factory and Chez Panisse are two of my favorites. They aren't alike. One is large and bustling, and the other is small and intimate. There's another difference.

The Cheesecake Factory menu reads like a

book. It's overwhelming. Chez Panisse has one selection; the chef decides what to make each
evening. The Cheesecake Factory's extensive
menu mixes and matches basic sauces and simple
ingredients in endless variations. Chez Panisse re-
lies on the excellence of local, fresh ingredients
and the creativity of the chef. Whether you prefer
to have unlimited options or just one choice, both
these approaches are sure to satisfy and delight.

I thought of the way God serves a menu of
choices in my life. Sometimes my life is the
Cheesecake Factory. He mixes and matches His
basic truths with what I need. I long to feel His
love, and someone appears offering the very thing
I crave. I pray for direction, and I suddenly remember a Bible verse, or just the right verse leaps
off the page as I read. If it's discipline I need, God
gives a life lesson. He serves me from His extensive menu of love, grace, forgiveness, comfort, discipline, and compassion in endless combinations.
But sometimes, like the chef at Chez Panisse, God
offers one choice—served His way.

Whether God gives me what I need in the moment, like the short-order cook at the Cheesecake
Factory, or whether He provides the same loving
truth elegantly presented like the chef at Chez
Panisse, God serves me the very best. He doesn't

sugarcoat the meal. He doesn't force me to eat what He provides, but I am not served something else. If I gorge on junk food, God will not chastise me into accepting His meal, even though He's disappointed with my choices. He will, however, offer His truth on a silver platter again and again until I recognize that what He offers is marvelous and savor it.

For the mountains may depart and the hills be removed, but steadfast love shall not depart from you, and my covenant of peace shall not be removed, says the LORD, who has compassion on you (Isa. 54:10).

Food for Thought

- What lesson is God trying to serve you today?

- Are you ready to sample His menu?

- Can you remember a time God gave you just the morsel you needed? How did you respond?

- God gives us just what we need to grow in faith. You may be the one offering your guests just what they need that day.

Savories

Life often rolls along in a steady repetition of work and play. It seems nothing big happens; life is made up of lots of little things. Each day seems like the day before. I get sucked into life's rhythm, and I don't take time to notice the tidbits of delight sprinkled around me. And there are plenty:

—fresh figs from the farmers' market

—clean, crisp sheets on my bed

—gas prices down a nickel

—a short wait in the checkout line

—a favorite song on the radio

—a ruby-red sunset with purple clouds

—a funny comic strip

—an unexpected phone call from a friend

—fresh flowers on the kitchen table

—a sleepy morning hug from my son

—the smell of autumn in the air

I savor tiny treats that flavor my days with sweetness. They take the tart out of my mood. They season my outlook with positive thoughts. These are the morsels God slips in my day. Little blessings.

God doesn't sugarcoat life, but He does spice things up with pleasant sensations. When I enjoy the goodies, I find it's easier to pass over the taste of bitterness that threatens to sour my world. God offers me a banquet of bite-size delicacies that keep me from simmering in bland, tasteless stew.

From the fullness of his grace we have all received one blessing after another (John 1:16).

Food for Thought

- What savories have you enjoyed today?

- What ordinary joys have you overlooked or been too busy to enjoy?

- God shares small joys with you. Do little things come to mind you could share with guests? Make a list, then try adding a little something to your next gathering. It could be favorite foods, special music, a party favor, or fresh flowers.

Study the Recipes

I love to try new recipes. My husband and son know I want them to be completely honest when they rate a new dish. If they like it, it's guaranteed to appear on the dinner table again. If they don't, they won't see it again. Sometimes, if a dish is just on the brink of being great, we try to decide what would make it better and give it a second chance.

New recipes are my way of experimenting. Some chefs cook by instinct, but I am not so gifted; I need a recipe. I read and reread the instructions to make sure I'm heading in the right direction. Details matter: chop or mince, simmer or boil, teaspoon or tablespoon. I check the recipe.

I confess that I am not so obsessed with the details of my faith life. Sometimes my efforts are half-baked at best. I am slow to rise and seek to expand my knowledge. A seasoned cook works hard in the kitchen, has practiced techniques, and tries the recipes of others. A mature Christian works hard and is on her way to mastering the disciplines of the Christian life. But what recipes did she follow?

The Bible shows us recipes that are just right for every occasion.

- How to Love? Try 1 Cor. 13. These verses list all the attributes of love and how to use them as God does in the world.

- Want a better prayer life? Look at Matt. 6:7-15. This verse is a recipe for prayer. It tells us how to praise God, give Him thanks, and ask for His mercy and protection.

- How to build more faith? Try Eph. 6:13-18.

Here you will find all the ingredients you need in the battle for a strong faith.

These passages and many others can become favorites you will want to taste again and again. God's Word is a feast; it will fill every hunger you have. It helps to study the recipes.

Dear Father, renew my desire to dive into your Word. Help me to seek your guidance first. Amen.

Food for Thought

- Do you have favorite recipes you repeat often? What verses do you cling to?

- Have you been looking for help in all the wrong places? Reconnect with God's Word. It may be as simple as subscribing to a daily devotional. There are many to choose from. See the resources section for a list.

My Cupboards Overflow

I'm embarrassed by the bounty in my cupboards. I go to the grocery store and purchase anything I want. I don't budget for the cost of a loaf of bread, gallon of milk, or bag of chips. I buy them without thinking. It is unsettling to me to know that many must budget to put food on the table, and some have no food at all. I am able to try new cereals, spreads, sauces, crackers, sodas, cookies, or ice cream flavors. I indulge in cherries whenever I feel like it. I purchase tiny pints of blueberries all summer. I'm embarrassed not so much by the food in my cupboards, I guess, but by my ungrateful spirit. I take food for granted.

Food is not the only abundance I take for granted. Hospitality is sometimes one of them. I find it easy to throw a big party, so I tend to forget the importance of a small gathering. I go over the top with an event, but sometimes don't think about the small welcome that would mean so much to a guest. I overdo. And the gathering becomes all about me and my house and my skills at pulling off a big shindig. I take my gift of hospitality for granted.

God has poured His abundance into my life. He's given me many blessings, from the food on my table to the peace in my heart. I am the steward of those gifts. Being a steward means sharing. All I pour out will flow back to me many times over. Taking my gifts for granted does not honor God. We are given much and expected to share, not hoard.

Give, and it will be given to you. A good measure, pressed down, shaken together and running over,

will be poured into your lap. For with the measure
you use, it will be measured to you (Luke 6:38).

Food for Thought

- Do you take your gifts for granted? What action can you take to help bring you a grateful heart? Prayer?

- How can you be mindful of using hospitality? How can you share your gifts?

Meat and Potatoes

My life is very meat and potatoes. Basic, ordinary, low on side dish excitement. When I listen to the potluck of spiritual testimonials, I feel I have nothing to offer. Do you ever feel this way? I do not have a knock-your-socks-off conversion-to-faith story. My mom and dad told me about God when I was little. I believed them, and my faith deepens over my lifetime.

I am caught thinking, *Why share my faith? No drama. No hook. Nothing to keep the audience riveted.* Instead, my story is slow and patient. God is a powerful force in my life, but there is not a dramatic "save." I get up every day and try. I try to let God lead. Not the stuff of Hollywood. I share my story just so others will know God will meet them wherever. He'll pull you out of the gutter, sure. But He'll also find you in the boring carpool lane or the busy fast-food line. God shows up for the ordinary as well as the extraordinary.

As you think about sharing your faith through hospitality, do you worry you will have nothing to say? Happy news: you don't have to say anything dramatic. You may have a faith story of miraculous conversion. If you are comfortable sharing it, by all means tell your story when you can. If you are like me, though, and have only the little things of daily living, share those. I find that many people overlook the little blessings. I watch for them. It's like sneaking a peek at God's glory. I know He's here; I just have to find Him. When you train your eyes, you will see Him everywhere.

Are you meat and potatoes like me? Do you yearn to be special but feel like leftovers? Here's a secret: you are special. God loves your simple meat-and-potato style. He knows there are many who will respond to your brand of hospitality. It's hearty and honest. Hospitality served up as an everyday dish is delicious. There is no need for banquet proportions of grandeur. Tell it like it is.

*When I came to you, brothers, I did not come with
eloquence or superior wisdom as I proclaimed to you
the testimony about God. My message and my
preaching were not with wise and persuasive words,
but with a demonstration of the Spirit's power*
(1 Cor. 2:1, 4).

Food for Thought

- Do you wish for a grand story and have only humble beginnings? Write out your faith story; don't pad the details. Tell it simply. Someone out there will relate to this very story.

- How can you find the simple beauty in living with God daily? Train yourself to look for the movements of God in your life.

- Hospitality does not mean you have to put on a show, it means you have to be yourself with your guests.

Get Off the Couch

One Monday morning, my sister Nancy called to tell me she'd had a miscarriage. This longed-for baby, the answer to years of prayer, was gone. We tiptoed around each other's tender feelings and broken hearts. As we talked on Tuesday, we remembered that I had planned to give a dinner party for Nancy on Friday. In spite of our sorrow, we decided to go ahead with our plans. I spent Wednesday shopping for the dinner party. Thursday I spent cooking. Friday we enjoyed the dinner party, and it was a needed distraction. On Saturday, Nancy and I escaped by spending the day window shopping.

Finally, on Sunday, I lay on the couch after church trying to muster the energy to put away all the party stuff, do the laundry, and buy groceries for the coming week. Nancy called to chat. I could tell she wanted to go for a walk. Not just a walk really—a hike in the lovely hills near where I live. "Well, okay," I said. "Sure."

I relate this story to share what it revealed to me. God is going to call me to do His work—even when I don't want to. Even when I'm tired and looking forward to spending time doing things that are important to me. I laughed a little. I remembered thinking "called to do God's work" meant going to Africa or working with the homeless. I've learned it also means being available to someone right in my own family.

We went for a hike. I bought enough groceries for dinner. I skipped the laundry. I changed my plans, not because I'm a martyr, but because God first offered me His grace and it was my turn to re-flect it back.

Dear Father, when my enthusiasm lags, nudge me off the couch. I want to shine your love into the world even when my energy level is low. Spark me with the joy of your presence and the desire to share it with others whenever you lead. Amen.

Food for Thought

- Think of a time you wanted to stay on the couch. How did you respond?

- Was there a nudge from the Spirit that got you going? What was it?

- Using the gift of hospitality requires some effort. What will get you moving to unwrap this gift?

It's the Best!

"Can I have the recipe?"

"Sure, it's so easy."

Women share recipes all the time. I think it should be a requirement to include the recipe with every potluck dish—especially those perennial fa-vorites. Someone will want it. Lunchtime talks at work often end up as discussions about what to make for dinner. Using a new idea I just heard about makes the evening go smoother.

I collect recipes. I trade them, compare them, and share them. I'm always searching for new ideas to try in my own kitchen or tracking down old favorites. It dawned on me recently that I don't talk about the gospel with the same level of enthusiasm as I hand out cooking ideas. I am quick to say, "These are the best cookies, here let me give you the recipe." I take more pleasure in giving out confetti cookies than I do in telling someone, "Hey, God loves you. In fact, God loves you so much He died to save you and now He wants to live in your heart."

The Good News is better than hot cookies and cold milk, yet I get more excited about the crumbs. It's hard for me to talk about my love of God. I get tongue-tied. Maybe the thing to do is share the Good News over a plate of cookies! Then the deeds I do will give wings to my words.

Dear Father, may our excitement for sharing the Good News burn with hot-out-of-the-oven enthusiasm. Amen.

Food for Thought

- Think of the times you were excited about

God, surprised by His actions, blessed by His grace. *Write out the story to help keep it fresh in your mind. It doesn't have to be your testimony.* In fact, it will be even better if it is a small thing that shows the faithfulness of God.

• Pray for an opportunity to share your excitement.

Confetti Cookies

2½ cups flour
1 tsp. baking soda
1 tsp. salt
1 cup softened butter
2 cups sugar
2 tsp. vanilla
2 eggs
4 cups Rice Krispies cereal
1½ cups Mini M&Ms

Combine butter, sugar, and vanilla until smooth. Add the eggs. Mix in flour, baking soda, and salt. Stir in Rice Krispies and M&M's. The dough will be stiff. Drop dough by teaspoon onto a cookie sheet. Bake for 12 to 14 minutes at 350°.

Something Smells Good

Smell is a strong memory trigger. The scent of mothballs instantly takes me back to Grammy Mabel's house on 8th Street. With the attic door open, the scent of mothballs pressed out on me. I never knew what treasures I might find in that attic.

The aroma of fresh bread is a comfort for many. It makes me think of favorite bakeries or the happy memory of my brother making brioche in our kitchen in Annapolis. He was home from cooking school and practicing on us. His brioche tasted even better than it smelled.

The salty tang of beach air . . . warm, clean blankets . . . construction paper and crayons . . . campfires . . . roses . . . cologne . . . Sunday morning bacon sizzling. Each sniff is a vivid memory.

We can be the aroma of Christ in the world. What does that mean? Waft into someone's life with the scent of Christ. Let the fragrance of your acts of love be a strong memory trigger for others.

A hot meal smells delicious to one who is hungry. A cheery card in the mail smells like friendship to a lonely shut-in. Cleaning a new mother's home whiffs of bleaching care. Rake a neighbor's yard and sniff the musty scent of assistance. Permeate the lives of those around you with the aroma of Christ. Like cologne lingering in a room, they will breathe it in and remember.

For we are to God the aroma of Christ among those who are being saved and those who are perish-

ing. To the one we are the smell of death; to the other, the fragrance of life. And who is equal to such a task? (2 Cor. 2:15-16).

Food for Thought

- Can you be the aroma of Christ? What small thing can you do to show Christ to someone?

- What is the fragrance of Christ in your life?

- Opening your home to guests is a wonderful opportunity to share Christ with others. Their time in your home will be a sweet memory. You can plant a seed of love.

Plan B

My brother is the chef in our family. He's been to cooking school. He's been a waiter in New York City for 20-odd years. I love to visit his home because of the tantalizing aromas. I watch, amazed, as he produces creations I would never attempt.

One year during the holidays he set out yummy nibbles that included spiced almonds. The almonds were so tasty that he had to refill the nut bowl several times as we gobbled them gone. After that visit, I found myself craving those nuts.

I called Brian for the recipe. He dictated as I jotted down ingredients and instructions.

"Yum. Thanks. I'll try these as soon as I can get to the store for supplies."

"Good luck."

Half an hour later the phone rang. "Lisa, those almonds are really a pain to make. I found another recipe for pecans. I think you'll have better luck with these."

"Well, okay." I was disappointed but took down the recipe. But I couldn't get those almonds out of my mind. Brian obviously thought I wasn't capable of conquering them. Well, I'd show him.

I bought the supplies for the spiced almonds. But making them was a time-consuming and frustrating process. Even though I followed the instructions carefully, they just didn't come out quite right.

So, . . . I bought all the supplies for the vanilla pecans. Although the instructions for this recipe were also very detailed, they were much easier to follow. Forty minutes later I was tossing the spices on the pecans and letting them cool.

I hated to admit my brother was right. Even with his expertise, he had found the almonds tedious to produce; maybe he'd just been trying to save me the hassle. Sibling that I am, I assumed he doubted my culinary skills.

I've been through this whole experience with God too. I ask for guidance, then pursue a path of my choosing that causes me frustration. I go back and try again, paying more attention to where I should be. Just as my brother was looking out for me when he suggested which recipe was a better choice for me, God looks out for me too.

God knows exactly where we are and what we're up to. He's ready to help us through the detailed instructions of any task before us. He doesn't doubt our abilities; to the contrary, He has tailor-made tasks to fit the abilities He gave us.

For we are God's workmanship, created in Christ Jesus to do good works, which God prepared in advance for us to do (Eph. 2:10).

God's gifts and his call are irrevocable (Rom. 11:29).

Food for Thought

- What tailor-made task does God have for you? If you're not sure, list skills you love to use. You might find your next step.

- What items on this list will enhance your gift of hospitality?

Vanilla Pecans

1 lb. pecan halves
½ cup sugar
2½ Tbsp. corn oil
1 Tbsp. vanilla

Put the nuts in boiling water for one minute. Stir and drain. While the nuts are hot, toss with the other ingredients. Spread in a single layer on a baking sheet and roast for 30 minutes at 350°. Stir the nuts every ten minutes so they don't stick and burn. Pour the hot nuts in a large bowl, sprinkle with the following mixture of spices:

½ tsp salt
¼ tsp each of pepper, coriander, cinnamon, nutmeg, and allspice

Spread the nuts on a clean surface to cool. Store in an airtight container.

Spicy Almonds

2 cups whole white almonds with skins, blanched
3 Tbsp. peanut oil
½ cup sugar

Heat the oil in a heavy skillet. Add almonds and sprinkle with sugar. Using a wooden spoon, stir constantly over medium heat until the almonds turn golden brown. Remove almonds to a bowl containing the following ingredients and toss:

1½ tsp. salt
1 tsp. cumin
1 tsp. hot pepper flakes
1 Tbsp. sugar

Spread the nuts on a clean surface to cool. Store in an airtight container.

The Oven

Ding. The first batch of Christmas sugar cookies was ready to come out of the oven. I grabbed a hot pad. The oven was cold. What a time for my oven to quit working! Cookies lined the counters ready to go in the oven for the cookie exchange the next day. I put in a desperate call to my neighbor who graciously preheated her oven. I began shuttling cookies back and forth. To say I was frustrated would be an understatement.

My cold oven sat empty into the New Year. It was time to replace the 35-year-old fixture, but with so many commitments at that time of year we couldn't find time to shop for a new one until mid-January. Finally, we made a selection and went home to confirm the measurements.

Monday afternoon I called to place the order. "We'll put the order in next Monday. We've already sent the Maytag order for this week." Delay number one. My wait for a working oven dragged on for four months. Everything that could go wrong, did. The oven was backordered and when one was finally delivered and installed, it was defective. Another wait. The truck bringing the replacement crashed. They delivered an electric model instead of gas. Delay after frustrating delay.

It seemed that every recipe I read started with *Preheat the oven to 350°*. I ran out of stovetop ideas, got tired of take-out, and the rainy season kept me from grilling. UGH! When the oven was finally successfully installed, it was almost anticlimactic. I was beaten.

I baked chicken for dinner that first evening. With the oven warm, I thought, "I'll pop in some banana bread." I went through the familiar motions of measuring and mixing. Yummy smells filled my kitchen again. I smiled. I had really missed baking.

Baking is something I do well, and it gives me great pleasure. I enjoy sharing treats. Baking is a simple gift. While I was without an oven, I felt I was being denied the opportunity to use part of my hospitality talent. That made me cranky, frustrated, and sad. I felt I'd missed opportunities to bring joy and pleasure to others. A couple of those others were my husband and son who wanted a home-cooked meal.

This experience allowed me to see how significant my simple talent is. Hospitality is an integral part of who I am. Yes, I can be gracious without offering a plate of cookies, but it feels incomplete.

We all have certain gifts and special talents. When we don't use them, we miss out. We flounder, searching in all the wrong places for something to do. And the world misses out on our unique offerings. Hospitality happens to be my gift; I want to use every aspect of it I can muster. Everyone has some measure of hospitality, and we honor God when we use that gift.

Dear Father, Thank you for giving me many gifts and blessings. Help me find ways to use these gifts for your glory. Amen.

Food for Thought

- What talents for hospitality do you have? Cooking? Decorating? Party planning? Good listening?

- What aspects of this total package excite you and make you want to get going right now?

- Are you missing opportunities to use your talents? If you want to dig deeper into finding your talents, Max Lucado's book *The Cure for the Common Life* is a great place to start.

Can We Try This, Please?

My son loves to help in the kitchen. Zach's 13 and can handle a knife, and he's becoming a pretty good sous chef (preps for the chef). Zach also loves to know how things work. He likes to tinker and tear apart, and he really likes to watch shows that tell him how it's done, whatever "it" is. When you marry these two interests, you get a big fan of *Good Eats,* a cooking show on the Food Network. The host, Alton Brown, demystifies cooking by explaining the science behind all those reactions, calculations, and combinations. He gets right down to the molecular level. The science of cooking is presented with flare and humor, and delicious creations are the result. When you follow these new lessons, your cooking becomes *Good Eats.* I'm a big fan of the show as well.

A recent episode focused on wonton wrappers. The basic premise of the show: take a chance on a new ingredient. My son was enthralled.

"Let's make those, Mom!"

"What? Potstickers? No! Those are for restaurants." Even though I'd just watched Alton whip up a batch with ease, my reaction was negative. But Zach would not be swayed.

"Let's do it. It'll be fun."

"Well, if you can find the wonton wrappers at the store, maybe."

I was counting on the store not stocking them. But on the next grocery trip, Zach found the wrappers, and I reluctantly purchased all the ingredients we needed.

Zach had taped the show, so we watched it one more time to be sure we were ready before we started the potsticker production. We measured, we mixed, we stuffed, and we folded just as instructed. They stuck to the pan perfectly, and they steamed free perfectly. They tasted perfect. We were *so* impressed with ourselves.

Zach turned to me and before he could even smirk, I said, "I never, and I mean *never*, would have tried this if you hadn't pushed me. These are wonderful. Thank you."

My son's youthful enthusiasm set the example, and he dragged me along for the delicious ride. It was only potstickers, but it got me thinking. What do I miss because I'm too intimidated to try? Have I lost all sense of adventure? Where's my enthusiasm? Lucky for me, there are all kinds of ways for God to reach into my life and get me going again. This time He used a child. This time He reminded me there is excitement everywhere

—in my kitchen, around the corner, and across the ocean.

For I know the plans I have for you, declares the LORD, plans to prosper you and not to harm you, plans to give you hope and a future (Jer. 29:11).

Food for Thought

- Have you lost your enthusiasm? Is God calling for you to take a look around? What do you see that is beyond your comfort zone?

- What intimidates you about opening your home to guests?

- What leap of faith could you take to overcome your stuck place? Try a small thing.

- If you'd like to try Alton Brown's potstickers, you can find the recipe on Foodnetwork.com. Search for "perfect potstickers."

2

Excuses, Excuses

Are you suffering from can't-have-anybody-over-itis? You know who you are. You'd really like to have guests, but you can come up with a million reasons why now isn't a good time. So what's on *your* list? There are several variations on the standard excuses for not putting out the welcome mat.

I will have people over as soon as
. . . I have my house ready for company. I don't know about your house, but at my house the kitchen table is a magnet for every stray piece of paper that finds its way in through the mail, a backpack, or a briefcase. Some evenings we eat dinner in front of the TV because of the clutter. I hate that, so I try to keep the table cleared.

Lack of clutter control keeps us from having people over. We tend to think the whole house needs to be neat and organized before we open our door. Guests are there to see you—not do an inspection. As a matter of fact, few guests go further than your kitchen, living room, and guest bath. So do yourself a favor and concentrate on those three areas. Unless you're hostessing an open house with guests invited to roam from room to room, you can count on them staying pretty much where you put them and where the food is.

Clear off a few counters, vacuum, and swish out the bathroom. That's the short list of manageable tasks. If the short list isn't going to do the trick, then I recommend the book *Too Much Stuff* by Kathryn Porter to help you get your clutter under control. Another great resource is www.flylady.net. Both of these are great tools that will help you change your life and your attitude if you're inclined to let your stuff own you rather than the other way around.

But for now you can start small by cleaning up those three rooms. If a nosy guest won't stay put, politely suggest he or she see the rest of the house another time. I've been known to throw every bit of unwanted clutter into one room and shut the door. Only a determinedly brazen guest will open a closed door. If you are worried—lock it!

. . . I have enough money. This is a valid excuse, but even a limited budget can stretch to entertain. Remember—it's about relationships. When my uncle was in medical school, he and my aunt lived in a tiny apartment above a drugstore. Another medical student and his wife lived across the hall. The two couples became good friends. In the evening they shared a lemonade or soda and enjoyed each other's company in one apartment, but at dinnertime the visiting couple headed home. Neither budget allowed for a meal for four.

A young couple I know moved into their first apartment. Excited to share their new digs with friends, they envisioned a housewarming party. The expense of moving and living in the city left money tight, though, so they had friends over in ones and twos, a couple for dinner, a pair for coffee, etc. It took longer to "warm" the apartment, but they had fun doing it.

Practicing hospitality does not require a big bank account. It's about building relationships, and all that requires is a willingness to be open to creative possibilities. Perhaps you can combine your resources with another hostess. Maybe potluck is an option. Sometimes I save up for a gathering in my home. I see hospitality as my personal ministry.

. . . I have learned to cook. Invited guests expect to be served *something*. Folks may know cooking is not your thing, but they know they'll be welcome at your house and they enjoy your company. So entertain with potluck, take-out, or even have something catered if finances are not an issue. Or you could ask everyone to bring an hors d'oeuvre and order in from a favorite restaurant. Or pick up one of those roasted chickens or a deli tray from your grocery store. And don't forget the grocery store bakery. See—you don't have to be a hostess who cooks; just be a hostess who cares and creates an environment where people can love and be loved.

If you really *want* to add cooking to your bag of hospitality tricks, take baby steps. Don't try a whole menu of new recipes. Try one new creation and fill in with other dishes that are tried and true. Ready-made dishes may be just the ticket for filling out your meal. Spending time on the entrée? Buy a yummy dessert this time, and keep your stress level low.

If you want to improve your culinary skills, consider taking a cooking class. My son and I took a sushi workshop at the Viking Home Chef store. We gained the confidence to try it at home. We still need practice, but what fun! The Viking Home Chef offers a variety of classes. Look them up online: vikinghomechef.com. For more ideas of what's in your area, call the food editor of your local paper.

. . . **I have more time.** In *Ferris Bueller's Day Off*, Ferris says, "Life moves pretty fast. If you don't stop and look around, you could miss it." Ask yourself where you can slow down. There is probably something you're committed to now that you don't enjoy and would like to give up (no fair saying the laundry). Are there time-wasters that could be eliminated? You'll find time when you examine your activities.

I discovered an hour when I can sneak away each afternoon. While my eighth grader does his homework, I have a coffee date or a walk with a friend. It's hospitality for one. Look closely at your daily schedule. You might find a bit of time you can put to better use.

Squeezing extra time out of each day requires deliberate action on your part. Look at next month's calendar. Where can you make some room? Look for a free Saturday morning or a couple of hours when the kids are in youth group meetings or Friday night pizza and movie. Maybe you could invite a few friends over after church. You don't have to set yourself up for every Sunday afternoon or second Tuesday evening of every month. Just try something once to see how it goes. Remember—it's about building relations, not about an elaborate production. Keep it simple, and you are likely to find the time.

It seems free time is never in ample supply. If we don't deliberately make time for things that are important to us, we will miss out on a lot. When I have more time I will . . . read, travel, sleep, exercise, study, write, sing, golf—fill in the blank—the list goes on and on. We only get 24 hours each day. Truth is, you make time for the things that are important to you. Start small; give an hour to exercising your hospitality muscle and see what happens.

. . . **I have completed the bathroom/kitchen/bedroom/fill in the blank.** This is your pride talking. Of course you want a pleasant environment for your guests, but waiting for the perfect house to entertain in is like putting off having kids until you can afford them. It may never happen. Are you interested in showing off your house or sharing your friendship and faith? When I was a new homeowner, I wanted to have people over nonstop. I was so excited to own a home that I overlooked boxes in the corner and rooms with little furniture. My excitement was contagious. My guests helped spark decorating possibilities and gave me great ideas.

In the early days, I invited guests because I was thrilled to be in my own home. Later, friends came during the mess. When we redid our son's room, we let visitors see the progress. Better than before and after pictures, we showed them during. They saw our progress, and the ultimate unveiling was more fun to share.

. . . **the kids are older.** When you have toddlers, there is never a good time for a dinner party—so don't have one. With young children at home, hospitality has a different look. You can include the kids by letting the playgroup meet at your house, having a backyard barbecue, or a movie night of classic cartoons. There will be time later for more grown-up entertaining. Don't miss out on the fun just because the living room floor is cluttered with toys and one of the hosts and some of the guests have to be in bed by seven. Your family can grow along with other young families. Share your hospitality with others whose situation is the same as yours.

. . . **I am a stronger Christian.** No one ever "arrives" on Christianity easy street. We will, hopefully, continue to mature in faith as long as we live. And it is such a rich experience to grow along with other Christians. Sharing the experiences of your walk with Christ with others strengthens your own convictions. And hearing their experiences brings the joy of a shared faith.

If your guests are not Christians, what they see taking place in your life may get them thinking about their own lives. As they see God moving in your life, they may begin to see that their own lives are not just happenstance. How exciting to play a part in newfound faith in Christ! Bring those who are struggling with their faith into your home for a safe place to explore their questions.

If you are a new Christian, don't hesitate to use your hospitality to establish relationships with those who've been in the faith for years. You will grow from their wisdom. Hostess does not necessarily mean teacher; what joy to gain insight from your guests. You will never have all the answers anyway, so don't wait.

At the end of the party, hospitality is not about the food, the house, the age of the guests, or the time and money you spent. It is about the guests and your willingness to welcome them with genuine warmth and affection.

Food for Thought

- Clutter. Money. Cooking. Time. Remodeling. Children. Bible knowledge. Which excuses hit home with you? Why?

- How are you hiding behind closed doors? What steps can you take to put excuses behind you?

Dear Father, I have put off sharing my faith and friendship with others. I use excuses to hide behind closed doors. Help me open my door to your people. Help me find ways to put these excuses to rest. Amen.

3

Come On In

Sharing your faith is really just opening your life to others and then being yourself. One good way to do this is to open your home. Hospitality is not a gift you open and use once and then put back on the shelf. The more you use your gift of hospitality, the more you will want to use it and the easier it will become to use it. You can give this gift to your family, your neighbors, and your community. It comes from your heart, and no one can give a gift exactly like the gift you give.

You can't entertain *wrong*. You welcome guests into your home with your own special touch. If an oddball idea pops into your head and it sounds like fun, give it a try. I'll be throwing out ideas that I think work for me; you may want to keep some of them and some of them will give you ideas of your own. Just jump right in and do your own thing. When you do it your own way, you'll have fun with it.

You might be wondering how to go about inviting friends or neighbors over. You may be trying to pinpoint the perfect occasion. You might be asking, *Will they be hungry? What will I do to keep them entertained??* You're probably wanting answers to the questions that buzz around in your head.

The Agenda

The movie *Searching for Bobby Fisher* is the true story of eight-year-old chess prodigy, Josh Baskin. Once his parents discovered his gift, Josh's father decided to get him lessons from a chess master. For the first lesson, the master came to the house and was introduced to Josh. The two are left alone in Josh's room for an hour. At the end of the lesson as the father is paying the teacher, he asks how it went.

"Fine. Fine."

"Did you talk about chess?"

"It didn't come up."

The father is stunned into silence and looks disbelieving as the teacher leaves saying he'll be back the next week. It didn't come up? Unbelievable! All that effort to arrange an environment for learning and it didn't come up? You can feel the father's unspoken question, *Then why in the world am I paying you?*

Several lessons follow where chess doesn't come up. In fact, the teacher and student play other games as they get to know each other. Eventually, Josh becomes well tutored by the master, and he finds his heart for the game.

Josh's father's agenda was to help his son become a chess champion. He thought the path was clear—find a teacher, put the student with the teacher, and get immediate results. The chess master had an agenda as well, it was to teach the student to love the game. The teacher was willing to wait patiently for the student's passion to develop until the student was ready to follow.

What is your agenda? You may want so much to share your faith that you push too hard. If you're not careful, guests may decline your invitations because they realize every visit to your home involves a Bible track, prayer meeting, or church discussion. It's perfectly okay if your faith isn't discussed every time you entertain guests. Your agenda can be to simply hang out, have fun, and enjoy your guests. The very fact that you open your heart and home sends a subtle yet powerful message. The subject of God may not come up, but He is always a guest at your table. The only agenda is not to have an agenda.

I've never thrown a party and talked faith all evening with my guests. In fact, I can't remember a time when an evening centered on God and how

important He is to me. If I'm asked to share my
faith it comes later, after the party's over.

One time a friend came to me and said, "I
know you pray. Could you pray about something
for me?" She'd been a guest in my home many
times. I'd never prayed for her around the dinner
table, and I'd never told her my faith story. I don't
remember even mentioning I go to church. But
she knew. From visiting with me often and being a
guest in my home, she knew she could ask me to
pray for her. How did she find out? There are
many clues in my home. She could have seen the
books and movies on my shelves. She heard me
talking about things that are important to me. She
could tell what matters to me by looking around
my home. She would have felt welcomed and
would have known I care about her. Did I tell her
I'm a Christian and that I'd be praying for her? No,
there was no agenda. It didn't happen after her
first visit to my home; she was a guest many times.
But I can't hide my faith any more than I can hide
being right-handed. Your hospitality can lead to
things you could not possibly plan.

For my 40th birthday party, I gathered 35 of
my nearest and dearest friends. It was a great
evening. The question of the night was, "How do
you know Lisa?" It became the conversation

starter for everyone. I had gathered my work friends, mommy friends, writer friends, church friends, and neighborhood friends. They all wanted to make a connection.

In the days after the party, friends said to me, "You have such great friends." I laughed, because each gal who said it was a friend of mine. I felt like saying, "I know. You're one of those great friends."

There were surprising connections among my friends. In fact, my friend Marilyn commented, "Who'd have thought I'd go to a white girl's birthday party and find a connection to the black community in Sebastopol!" During the evening Marilyn struck up a conversation with Sue. They discovered that Sue knew some ladies in Sebastopol where Marilyn had recently moved. As it turns out, Sue was the connection to the African-American community that Marilyn was seeking. I couldn't have planned that.

Sharing your faith means opening your life to people and then being yourself with them. You cannot control how it happens, when it happens, or even if it happens. You just provide the environment and be yourself.

Food for Thought

- Do you have an agenda? What is it?

• What are your ideas about hospitality? Do you think your ideas match God's plan for using the gift of hospitality?

• Are you willing to take God's lead on this adventure in hospitality? How can you sit back and be yourself?

The Full Spectrum

My neighbor Silvia does not enjoy cooking, yet she is the first one to invite the neighbors in for a potluck. She's great at creating community. She opens the door, orders pizza, and asks the folks on the block to bring the rest.

We visit and catch up on each other's lives. We don't necessarily share our faith stories; however, we make connections. We get to know the folks who live right next door. These connections go a long way. In times of joy we'll be able to share a new job or a new baby or new bike. In times of stress it will be easier to reach out to each other and ask for help. *Can you watch my child after school? I'm sick. Can you stop at the grocery?* It's the perfect outcome from a neighborhood potluck. There's no big agenda; just living in community and shining love in that community. Be yourself.

The neighborhood potluck is just one place to

start. It's casual and doesn't require much planning. What if you want to make a bigger production out of your newfound gift of hospitality? Now things are really going to get interesting.

For me and many other hostesses, planning is half the fun. I planned my 40th birthday party for three years! Okay, so that's extreme, crazy even, but I had such fun thinking about it. I would go over the guest list and add more and more names of friends I wanted at the celebration. I would find little party favors and slowly collected them over all those months. I kept my eye out for unique recipes and tried them out so they would be well tested by party day. I had such fun planning the surprises I was sure my friends would enjoy. (More on those party specifics in the next chapter.)

So those are both extremes of party planning. You can give a no-plan party or a long-term-plan-ahead party. You probably want to start somewhere in the middle, right? Test the waters and see how this whole hospitality thing works? Fair enough.

In the Beginning Was the Invite

First, you'll want a reason for folks to come over. It can be as simple as you just want to touch base and get a few friends together, or it can be more elaborate. There are so many reasons to have folks in: girls night, dinner for six, movie night, back-to-school, off to college, new job, new house, new couch, birthdays, anniversaries, welcome new neighbors, invite new pastor, relatives in town, pool party, and of course, holidays. The list goes on and on, and any reason will do. It's Tuesday the 12th! Great, come on in! People love an excuse to get together. Let your house be the spot.

Drop-in entertaining is fun and spontaneous. "There's plenty. Why don't you stay?" But sometimes you plan in advance and for that you need invitations.

Remember, I mentioned in the beginning of the book there are several levels of entertaining: simple, special, and sumptuous. This applies to inviting your guests. The simple way is calling them on the phone, or you can contact them via e-mail. You can also try evite.com. That Web site has all kinds of invitations for every occasion. If you still haven't thought of an excuse for a party, search this site. It has all kinds of suggestions with invitations to match.

And don't forget that you can always invite your guests by snail mail. These days, it's such a surprise to get a friendly card in the mail along with all the junk. Sending invites in the mail will get their attention. You can pick out something simple at the drugstore or card shop and write the cards by hand. Or you can make a flyer on your computer. Clip art is a great addition. Of course, there's a Web site to get you started on that—clipart.com.

The sumptuous way to invite your guests is to make your own invitations. I love paper supplies, office supplies, and stationery stores. Invitations give me an excuse to go to the scrapbooking store and buy unique paper and decorative trinkets. These stores really get my creative juices flowing. I once fell in love with an unusual envelope and designed invitations around it. Extreme, I know. Just using pretty paper makes the cards unique.

If arts and crafts don't appeal to you, but you still want to indulge on spectacular invitations, you can have them designed for you. Ask at the stationery or paper supply stores. A sumptuous online resource for invitations is dauphinepress.com. Graphic designer Trish Kinsella offers wonderful letterpress creations printed on an old press with beautiful results. She's reviving a centuries-old craft.

On the invitation let your guests know as many particulars as possible. The occasion. Time. Date. Location. Is there going to be a full meal or just munchies? Don't assume they can tell from the time the party is being held. If they arrive at seven o'clock and have already had dinner, all your lovely food could go to waste.

What kind of attire do you expect? Is this fancy dress, Sunday best, or do you want them to show up in their sweats and slippers? It's hard to get a costume together at the last minute. Tell your guests what's going on. If it's no big deal, you don't even need to mention this. But if you have a tone you want to set, let them in on it. Everyone is more comfortable knowing. They'll look forward to coming!

Time and location are a must. If your event requires that everyone be on time for a presentation or dinner at a certain hour, let them know. Every year my nephew's birthday party happens on the weekend we change the clocks back to standard time. My sister-in-law always remembers to make a note of this on the invitations. Guests will be on time this way, not an hour early.

Does everyone know how to get to the party site? Include a map or directions, which are easy enough to provide with the Internet to help you out. Try Mapquest and Google maps. And don't forget the RSVP. If you are planning for fun, you've got to know how many folks will be there. If people don't RSVP, I call to ask if they can come. A week before the event is fair.

Feed Me!

A mom and toddler visited a friend's home. They stayed for a week. One day, while the hostess was off at a meeting, the toddler got hungry, so Mom went into the kitchen to look around. How about some cereal? No Cheerios, just Grapenuts and skim milk. How about some juice? Only guava. Cheese and crackers? Bleu cheese, goat cheese, or brie on rye crisps. Fruit? Figs. Lots of food, but there was nothing kid-friendly in the whole kitchen.

Know your guests and cater to them. You don't have to stock everything they *might* like, but know who you are serving and be appropriate. Is one of your guests a vegetarian? Does anyone have a food allergy? If you are unsure, ask. It will make everyone more comfortable.

The day my son lost his first front tooth I served corn on the cob for dinner! Oops. He burst into tears after the first bite. That was one of his favorite things, and he couldn't eat it. I wasn't sensitive to his needs. Your guests may not burst into tears because of something you serve, but it's wise to be thoughtful of them.

I have a junk drawer at my house for kids who come to visit. It's where I store the chips, fruit snacks, nuts, and other kid-friendly goodies. Of course, they all know the drill, eat something healthy first! Grab yogurt or a piece of fruit and then, if you are still hungry, check out the junk drawer. I have a self-serve policy now that my son and his friends have hit the teen years. They are well trained; they still grab something healthy first.

Food, like everything else, goes in and out of fashion. We are all more health conscious than we used to be. When planning your menu, think of foods that are both simple and a little sinful. Offering a low calorie feast is great, but dress it up. It's a party; it's time to treat yourself and others to a little something special. Presentation can make what you're serving look as wonderful as it tastes. If you're planning high-calorie fun, keep the portions small.

First, decide on the main dish—the featured item. It can be a simple crock-pot dish, a special family recipe, or a sumptuous gourmet offering. Where does your expertise lie? Keep the party prep within your comfort zone. Once you plan the main dish, think of complementary tastes. Balance the flavors—not all spicy or all mild. A mix will let all the flavors come through.

The menu can go something like this: Appetizers can be simple cheese and crackers or sumptuous asparagus wrapped with prosciutto. Soup or salad gives me an excuse to try out a new soup recipe and give each guest a small serving. The entree or main course is served with veggies, potato, rice, and/or rolls. Dessert—well, other than your friends at the table, dessert is the best part of the event.

Next, think of what you'll be able to do ahead. Not every dish should be made the day of the party. Balance your menu for preparation times as well as flavors. Serve a soup you can make a day or two ahead. Try a dessert from the local bakery or plan a simple sorbet and bakery cookies that take no time. Not everything can go in the oven at once, so stagger your plan. Timing the food is something that takes practice.

Looking for tasty ideas? I have been building my library of cookbooks, but I stick to the tried-and-true more often than not. When I want to branch out I go to the library or surf the net and browse for recipes. The Web is a fantastic resource that offers complete menus and how-tos. Type an ingredient into a search engine and ask for a recipe. You'll find hundreds of ideas.

I like to keep my eye out for unique tastes and treats. There are lots of ready-made dishes that will fill out a buffet table or spice up a dinner party. Often, as I do the weekly shopping, I check out the latest and I keep an eye out for the unusual. For example, one week at our farmers' market I stopped by the cheese lady's booth to taste something called Lemon Quark. It's a delicious, sweet cheese spread that's wonderful on strawberries, crackers, or gingersnaps. I slowed down for a sample, and now it's a favorite taste I like to include at parties.

Another example of keeping my taste buds alert for the unusual came in our local sandwich shop. The sandwiches there are served on home-made bread, and I commented on how delicious I thought it was. Come to find out, they sell it by the loaf. I'm not a bread maker, so it was quite a treat to serve my guests warm, fresh, homemade bread. So slow down as you motor through your day; there might be new tastes to sample at the grocery store or quick tips to be found in magazines. Little surprises for your guests take some planning. If you keep you eyes open, you'll find things to de-light them.

If preparing food is not one of your pleasures, remember that you can find ways around it. Your plan can be to use a caterer, have a potluck, or or-der the pizza! It's entirely up to you. The food is just one slice of hospitality. Spend time hustling in the kitchen if you enjoy it, or spend time creating a mood and waiting to open the door for the caterer or potluck.

Potluck

Potlucks are the absolute easiest way to stage a party. What an easy entry into hospitality—you share the duties of food preparation with your guests. This gives you time to try some other touches to make your event unique.

Here are some potluck tips to remember.

Choose a particular type of potluck. Everyone brings a salad. Appetizers only. Make a favorite family recipe and bring it. Or assign some dishes; as folks RSVP let them choose what they'd like to contribute—appetizer, salad, side dish, main dish, or dessert. Keep track so there's a balance.

For those on your guest list who are cooking impaired, ask them to bring the drinks or a loaf of bread or condiments such as pickles, olives, or baby carrots.

As hostess, you'll need to provide utensils, cups, plates, silverware, and napkins. Remember to be ready for the chef who forgets a serving spoon or needs to heat something at the last minute. Have a spot prepared for drinks and ice. And so you don't end up with all the leftovers, have some disposable containers on hand so guests can take small servings home. Finally, ask folks to bring the recipe for the dish they are sharing.

Set the Stage

Once the food issue is settled, you can turn your attention to the house. Use all your senses when getting your home ready to entertain. Think about not only what your guests will see, but also what they will smell, taste, touch, and hear.

Once the house is presentable, you can add some extra visual touches. Fresh flowers are on my grocery list every week; I buy a cheap bunch for the kitchen table. It's an easy addition that the whole family enjoys. Another visual touch is lighting. I have a set of white Christmas lights I like to put up around the perimeter of the ceiling in the party room. I use masking tape to keep the lights in place for the evening. It's brighter and safer than candles. Splurge next December 26 when the after-Christmas sales hit, and treat yourself to a set of lights just for fun. Measure the perimeter of your room first. I over-purchased and came home with enough lights for three rooms. Oops.

Another look to try is handmade papers. Rather than having lots of tablecloths, I have a plain white one I dress up with special paper. I told you I love the scrapbook store, so any excuse to browse! These stores often display large sheets of handmade paper. I buy two or three sheets to complement my theme or color scheme and use it to dress up my buffet or dining table. When the party's over I recycle the paper by using it as gift wrap or cutting off any stains and spills and chopping the rest into invitations for the next gathering.

For me, decorating the table is such fun. Just about anything can be used. Flowers or anything natural is always a safe bet. Candles are popular as well. You can find ideas in magazines and on Home and Garden TV. For an autumn buffet table, I placed four pumpkins in the middle of the table and carved them out as vases. Inside each pumpkin I put a vase filled with flowers. I saw this idea in a magazine. Did my table look as professional as the glossy magazine pages? No, but it looked so cool in the magazine I wanted a reason to try it. Be brave when you see something you like and give it your own flare.

Let me share a word about centerpieces. It's fun to decorate a table with the theme of the season. Flowers, figurines, candles, all kinds of things can grace your table. However, be sure your guests can still see each other when they are seated. If the middle of the table holds a barricade of foliage, no one will be able to talk around it.

I let my son help get the table ready. When he was little and still into coloring all the time, I let him decorate paper placemats for our table. This was an especially good distraction for him on Christmas Eve when he was trying so hard to wait for Santa. It took him quite a while to illustrate all the placemats we needed.

Finally, your table will be complete with place cards. This is a fun addition and makes everyone feel special. This gives you a chance to seat guests together who would enjoy getting better acquainted. You can buy place cards at the stationery store. I have fun making them. First, the simple idea: cut and fold construction paper, put on a fun sticker, and write each guest's name. Special: buy fancy paper and clip several layers together with a specialty brad. Calligraphy each name. For the sumptuous: fill little bags (cloth or paper) with a tiny treasure (mints, coins, a tea light candle, etc). Tie each bag with a lovely ribbon and tag it with the guest's name. You have a party favor and place card all in one.

Can you remember visiting someone in December who had a real spruce in the living room? It just *smells* like Christmas, doesn't it? What aroma will greet people at your door? You can set the mood through the sense of smell. Food cooking? Candles burning? Fresh flowers from your garden? Cozy fire in the fireplace? Garlic is even a great greeting if the menu is an Italian feast.

What will your party sound like? Music in the background creates a party atmosphere. Is this a 50s celebration? Break out Elvis or Chubby Checker. For a casual dinner gathering, have quiet instrumentals in the background. You can even set the mood for a kids' party by playing tunes that fit. Wind them up, but be sure to have some tunes to calm 'em down too. We used to end my son's birthday parties with a Disney flick. Spy party: *Great Mouse Detective*. Pirate party: *Peter Pan*. Stargazing party: *Fantasia*.

Don't forget to think about how comfortable your guests will feel in your home. Is there enough room for everyone? Our kitchen table will hold only eight. I like serving buffets so I don't have to limit my guest list. Think about where guests are going to eat. If your gathering is not a food fest, think about where conversations can take place. Are you all going to gab in a big group? Is a circle of chairs necessary to make discussion easier? Or is the event one for meeting and mingling? You will want a few chairs here and there. Have a clear path around the food. Finally, give a thought to the temperature. More than once I have had to open windows in the winter to cool down the house. If you are going to have a full house, all those bodies will warm up the room, so turn down the heat.

Now What?

The food is planned, the house is clean, and we're ready to welcome our guests. Now what? If hospitality is a gift you love, this moment will be exciting. If entertaining makes you nervous, you may be tempted to pretend you aren't home and hope they go away! Come on, let them in, you'll all have a good time. It's finally time to enjoy your company. This is the fun part. The work of getting ready is over, now you can play with your friends.

Remember the story of Martha in the Bible? Jesus and his disciples are in town and Martha opens her home to them. Martha runs around getting everything ready. Then she complains to Jesus about her sister Mary who is enjoying the guests and not helping in the kitchen. "'Martha, Martha,' the Lord answered, 'you are worried and upset about many things, but only one thing is needed. Mary has chosen what is better, and it will not be taken away from her'" (Luke 10:41).

Ouch, put in her place by the Lord himself. I bet Martha still grumbled, "Yeah, but she gets to do the fun stuff while I have to get dinner on the table. It's not going to serve itself." Take a deep breath, Martha. Think this through. Guests are the most important ingredients to any gathering. If you don't have time for your company, what's the point? Will they feel welcome if you put them off till dinner is served? Hospitality is not effortless; there is some planning involved. But with repetition, you will become adept at putting visitors first.

Be patient with yourself. You are learning a new skill. With practice, your hostess skills improve. You'll have things ready to go by the time you open the door. You'll learn to keep an eye on glasses that need to be refilled or empty plates that need to be cleared. Each time you entertain, it gets a little easier to divide your attention just enough to see things are moving smoothly. I still mess up this part because I'm busy visiting with my friends. I take a long time getting everything ready; it's part of the joy for me. But once the guests arrive, I want to visit rather than check the punch bowl. Happily, I've made my guests at home and they are comfortable getting another drink or second serving on their own. Still, Miss Manners would not approve, so learn to keep an eye on your guests and see to their needs.

It's a good idea to learn the lesson of taking joy in your guests. You may not always get to prepare ahead of time. Parties may occasionally just happen at your house. That's what happened to Zacchaeus, remember? "When Jesus reached the spot, he looked up and said to him, 'Zacchaeus, come down immediately. I must stay at your house today.' So he came down at once and welcomed him gladly" (Luke 19:5-6). Are you ready for a visitor to come right now? I'd be a little nervous. However, the pangs of what to do are eased by knowing that I really just want to be with my friends. I don't have to worry about what we'll eat or how the house looks, because being with my friends is what's important. They come to see me, not my house.

My friend Barb comes over for lunch every now and then. No advance warning. We have only the lunch hour, so I don't spend our time together worrying about the dishes in the sink or the papers on the kitchen table. I clear off a spot and enjoy catching up with my friend. Our busy schedules of kids, work, and chores don't allow for lots of free time to connect. We've found this tidbit of time to spend together. I would miss a very rich friendship if I worried about the clutter in my house.

Let's Talk

What will you do with your guests? Talk? Visit? Share stories or catch up? You might even play a game.

Conversation is a dance. It requires the partners to take turns: talk and listen. Listening can be the richer half of conversation. I learn from my guests by listening. When guests are in your home you want them to feel like the center of attention. You went to the trouble of inviting them; it's time to get to know them better. I really love to talk, but I am learning to be a better listener.

Keep in mind some general rules of conversation.

Don't gossip. When people come into your home, they want to know they're safe. They want to know they won't be listening to gossip and that they're safe from being the subject of gossip at your next party. If you talk about others, let it be chatter that builds them up or recognizes their good qualities. Never delight in another's misfortune.

Move beyond the mundane. If you spend your whole time talking about the weather or the health of everyone present, everyone will be bored. Make an effort to start beyond those points. If the weather is such a safe opener that you can't get out of the habit, how about asking what a guest is planting in the garden now that the weather is warming? Or how you miss the plants of spring and are looking forward to their return. Complaining about the rain is tedious. I, for one, love the rain and look forward to that season.

Try a conversation starter. I attended a ladies night out, and we all had to bring our own mug, teacup, or glass. We were asked to share the story of our cup. "It was just the one I grabbed on the way out the door!" "This is my grandmother's." Some comments went beyond teacups. We all learned a little more about each other.

Here's another conversation starter: Tell us your full name and what you like or don't like about it. Simple enough question on the face of it, yet it led to intriguing tales of how names were given, why they were adored or hated, and naming our own children. This starter opened many avenues of conversation, and our afternoon passed with little known tidbits being revealed.

Everyone has a story. My husband's favorite question when he's at a loss for conversation is to ask the person to tell his or her bike story. If they stare at him blankly, he gives them a conversational nudge, "I used to love putting a card in the spokes." It gets them remembering what they loved about biking as a kid. Seems everyone has a bike accident or adventure they can remember.

Playing "Remember When" can be a great way to get things going. If you are stuck on the weather, try rainy days or snow days when you were a kid. You might hear about waiting for the school closing announcements on a frozen Minnesota morning or hurricane watch in Mississippi. These are far more intriguing than one more complaint about the weather, and you've shared a little of your life with each other. You can maneuver the conversation to things of interest rather than the ordinary comments about the weather.

Let it flow. I spent a very interesting evening once listening to each woman in a group tell how she met her mate. (If you try this, first be sure each person has a mate and can join in the conversation.) As each woman told her story, the others were intrigued. When one gal told of meeting her husband at a conference, we spent some time talking about conference experiences. Another husband was a musician, and we learned more about the music industry. Each account opened up another avenue to explore before the next gal told her story.

This was not something the hostess planned. During our small talk, we started commenting about what our men were up to while we were out with the girls. Husbands were watching the kids; boyfriends were playing cards with their buddies. "My husband hasn't changed since we met," one gal commented. Another woman was curious and asked "How did you meet?" That's how that conversation began. Go with it when a happy accident falls in your lap.

Don't abruptly change the topic. Let conversation flow naturally from one topic to another. Don't interrupt someone's story with your own agenda of what you'd like to talk about. Of course, never interrupt someone midsentence or derail them to the point they can't finish their thoughts. Sometimes, though, the conversation stalls and you steer it in a new direction. I've been known to say, "Hey, abrupt change of topic," and launch into an idea that struck me.

Don't monopolize the conversation. You can get conversations going, but don't hog the spotlight. You want to hear from your guests. The idea is to let your guests shine and feel comfortable and willing to share their lives with you.

Be an active listener. Show a genuine interest in your guests' stories and ask reasonable questions, but use common sense and don't ask intrusive questions. Listening to your guests will also give you clues to ways you can pray for them.

Let the Games Begin

If everyone is talked out and you want to try a little something different, play a game. I realize some people really hate party games. But if your guests are willing, be sure you choose games where no one is singled out or embarrassed.

Your local toy store is packed with group games. Specialty game shops are also good places to look if you want to find something really unusual. And, of course, you can always go online for games to complement any theme or situation. If you go online, be prepared to sort through some pretty raunchy suggestions before you find something that works for you.

In my little family of three we don't have enough players for many games, so when we have company and the time is right, we pull out a game from the cupboard. We particularly love Apples to Apples. Older kids can join in the fun of this one. It's a game of hilarious comparisons. It promotes giggling and silly conversation. Other games we have on hand are Outburst, Trivial Pursuit, Scrabble, Pictionary, Mad Libs, and Cosmic Wimp Out.

Cosmic Wimp Out is an inexpensive dice game that is easy to learn and silly to play. When I was learning I was sure they were changing the rules at every turn, but once you see the method to the madness, it's great fun. A basic set of cubes is only $3.50. You can purchase it online at cosmic wimpout.com

When my husband was in graduate school, money was tight, but Saturday night was usually pizza and Pictionary. We still laugh over those days with our Pictionary buddies. I urge you to put aside your artistic fears and give it a try.

My son and my nephew are crazy for Mad Libs. It's a fill-in-the-blank game that's hilarious. After years of playing it, we still enjoy it. You can get it online by going to us.penguingroup.com and search Mad Libs. You will find just what you need.

Follow My Lead is a fun game that requires no equipment and nothing to purchase at all, and it's fun for all ages. It works really well at a sit-down dinner. Select one guest to leave the room for a moment. Then select one guest at the table to be the leader. When the player returns to the table the leader will start some little movement such as tapping the edge of his or her glass with one finger or rubbing his or her hands together. Everyone else at the table follows the leader. When the leader changes movements so does the rest of the table. They may switch to rubbing their chins or scratching their ears. The player from out of the room gets three chances to guess who the leader is. The trick is to not get caught changing moves.

Another idea is a questionnaire. French talk show host Bernard Pivot invented this one and

James Lipton made it famous on the television show *Inside the Actors Studio*. It's entertaining and sure to spark some conversation. All you need are some index cards or paper and pens for everyone. Then ask these questions:

What is your favorite word?

What is your least favorite word?

What turns you on creatively, spiritually, or emotionally?

What turns you off?

What sound or noise do you love?

What sound or noise do you hate?

What profession other than your own would you like to attempt?

What profession would you not like to do?

What would you like to hear God say when you arrive at the Pearly Gates?

Say Thank You

As you know, when you have been the guest it is nice to call the hostess the next day and thank her for a lovely evening or write her a note. What a nice switch it is to thank your guests for coming with a written note. As I was writing this book I invited friends into my home to talk about hospitality or I interviewed them over coffee at a coffee shop. The next day I wrote to each one thanking her for coming and letting her know I valued her input and why her participation was helpful. It's become a happy habit to thank those who've come to visit.

Some idea starters for your note:

I'm glad you could join us; I hope you can come again soon.

I loved having you as a guest and I hope we'll have many more opportunities to visit.

If writing a note seems forced to you, a quick phone call is good too.

Time for Good-byes

Some evenings when the conversation is good, it's hard to say good-bye. I'm a night person, so I could chat until the wee hours. Usually my guests have to leave earlier than I would like. There are those times, though, when the guests don't show any signs of leaving and you're worn out. Maybe the invitation said the party would end at nine and they're still there at eleven. What should you do?

First, assess the situation. Does your guest really need to finish discussing something urgent with you, or is it idle chatter that could go on indefinitely? If you sense that your friend needs to talk, try your best to hang in there just a little longer. But if you can't resolve the need, suggest that you both sleep on it and continue the discussion tomorrow.

If, however, you're engaged in idle chatter that you're ready to end, look for an opening and suggest, "Next time we'll plan to visit longer. It's been a lovely evening, and we really have to do this again."

Time to Clean Up

You've had a great time, but the party's over. Believe it or not, I even like this aspect of entertaining. As I'm picking up plates, putting away leftovers, and loading the dishwasher, I'm also thinking about the evening. My husband and I talk about how things went. "Wasn't that a funny story so and so told?" "I was sorry to hear about so and so's troubles." "I didn't know so and so could juggle!" We enjoy bits and pieces of the evening all over again. When I switch out the light and head down the hall, there's one more thing I think about. I mentally sort through the guest list for those who might need a special prayer or thought before I turn in. I'm thankful to use my gift of hospitality.

4

Let's Party!

Maybe the hospitality bug has bitten you by now and you're intrigued enough to want some specific party ideas and how-tos—maybe something beyond the basic potluck. Maybe you'd like to get some ideas on throwing a grown-up birthday party. No problem. I've also got a few thoughts on other kinds of parties you can host. A hike. A barbecue. A house cooling. An art show. A road trip. And what about a party with a purpose? Giving to charity is fun and festive when you test out some new ideas.

In this chapter we'll get down to some specifics with party ideas, both large and small, you will want to try. You'll be sending out invitations by the time you're done reading!

The Spa Party

Girls' Night Out is a very popular theme. Women's ministry teams do it, college friends do it, coworkers do it. Why not do it at your house? First, think of a few friends who could really use a night off with no worries or family obligations.

Best to keep the guest list small so you can all relax. If anyone asks to bring something, tell them it's all taken care of. This is your chance to pamper your friends.

The *simple* spa plan is to choose the date, then call your friends. Next, rent a chick flick, bake a pan of brownies, and ask everyone to wear their slippers. Get comfortable for an evening of girl talk.

The *special* spa plan calls for a few more feminine touches. Find some girlie invites—cute note cards from the stationery store will do—and send them out in the mail. Give your guests at least two weeks notice. Plan some special food. You can offer girlie finger foods. Here are some recipes:

Deviled Eggs
    6 eggs
    3 to 4 Tbsp. light mayonnaise
    1 to 2 Tbsp. prepared mustard
    1½ Tbsp. pickle juice from sweet gerkins
    ½ tsp. garlic powder
    salt to taste

Place the eggs in a medium saucepan and cover with cold water. Bring to a boil, then reduce heat to a simmer for 10 to 15 minutes. Plunge the eggs into cold water to stop the cooking. When the eggs have cooled, remove the shells. Slice the eggs lengthwise, removing the yolks to a small mixing bowl. Set the whites aside. Add mayonnaise, mustard, and pickle juice to the yolks, mix thoroughly. Add garlic powder and salt to taste. If the mixture is too thick, add more pickle juice; if too thin, add more mayo. Fill the hollow of each egg white with the yolk mixture. If desired, garnish with parsley, tarragon, or paprika.

Garlic Savories

2 heads of garlic, cloves separated and peeled

1 cup heavy cream

1 tsp. salt

½ cup Japanese panko bread crumbs (or unseasoned white crumbs)

2 Tbsp. grated parmesan cheese

In a small saucepan over low heat, slowly cook garlic and cream until the garlic is soft enough to mash with a spoon, about 45 minutes. The cream will thicken and reduce. Remove from heat and mash the garlic with a fork. Add salt, panko, and parmesan, mixing well.

To use as a spread: Slice a baguette into thin rounds. Spread each slice with garlic mixture. Arrange on a baking sheet and place under broiler for 3 to 5 minutes or until they begin to turn golden brown.

To use as a stuffing: Remove the stems from 24 large button mushrooms. Fill each mushroom with the garlic mixture. Bake at 450° for 15 minutes till tops begin to brown. Let stand for 5 to 10 minutes before serving.

Every spa party needs an ample supply of chocolate. Skip dinner, start later, and have a chocolate buffet. Make brownies, buy boxed chocolates, serve hot chocolate, get a chocolate ice cream cake, maybe even splurge and rent a chocolate fountain! And here's a dark suggestion: order some frozen hot chocolate mix from Serendipity3 in New York, online at Serendipity3.com. It's a delicious piece of chocolate history. Or try these brownies. They're a little extra work but so worth it.

Malted Glazed Brownies
¼ cup flour
6 oz. package semisweet chocolate chips
¾ cup sugar
1 tsp. vanilla
2 eggs
⅔ cup flour
¼ tsp. baking powder
¼ tsp. salt
¼ cup malted powder
¼ cup milk

Glaze
⅔ cup milk chocolate chips
¼ cup heavy cream
2 Tbsp. malt powder
1½ tsp. light corn syrup

Line an 8 x 8 pan with foil and grease the foil. In a small bowl, combine malted powder and milk and set aside. In a large saucepan over low heat, melt semisweet chips and butter, stirring constantly. Remove from heat. Add sugar, vanilla, and eggs; mix well. Add flour, baking powder, and salt; mix well. Finally, add malted milk mixture, mix until smooth. Pour batter into prepared pan. Bake at 350° for 35 to 45 minutes or until the middle is set and a toothpick comes out clean. Let brownies cool in pan for 15 minutes then peel off the foil and cool completely on a rack.

Prepare glaze. In a small saucepan, combine milk chocolate chips, cream, malt powder, and corn syrup, and melt together over low heat until smooth. Remove from heat and let stand until the glaze has thickened but is still pourable.

Place brownies on serving plate. Pour glaze over the top of the brownies, spreading evenly, and let it dribble down the sides. Let stand until set, then cut into 36 squares.

Add some spa touches to your special evening. Set up a lotion bar. Put out five or six kinds of wonderfully scented creams for your guests to sample. Display them on a lovely tray or separate table covered with a linen cloth. Light your home with candles and place fresh flowers everywhere; think beyond the centerpiece of your food table. How about flowers in the bathroom, by the front door, or on the mantle?

The *sumptuous* spa party plan pulls out all the

stops. In addition to chocolate, lotions, flowers, and finger foods, there are party favors and activities. Hire a manicurist to give your guests a polish. Or a masseur to rub tired shoulders, backs, or toes.

Give party favors. I love an excuse to pick up little notions. When you see a little inexpensive treat in your shopping travels, buy it: mini sizes of luxurious lotions, a pretty hankie, a little book of quotes and encouragements, a sample box of chocolates, candles, bookmarks, picture frames. Have an assortment on hand; they don't all have to match.

When you've assembled a collection of goodies, wrap each gift in pretty paper and special ribbons. Again, no need for everything to match—use what's in your closet. Put a number on the gift tag of each treat. Have your guests pull a number from a hat to decide who gets each gift and open them together. Be prepared for a little trading. Or just let your guests pick a treat as they leave the party.

The Girlie 40th Birthday Party

As I mentioned earlier, I planned my 40th birthday party for three years. Every time I found a little something I wanted to do, I'd tuck the idea in the file. When it was finally time to get to work, I had more ideas than I could use.

I was celebrating with girlfriends, so I could have girlie food. And what do girls really want? DESSERT! The menu was soup and dessert. I made four kinds of soup, one for each burner on the stove. And then I had a banquet table full of desserts. It was a delicious success. I labeled each soup and dessert with a place card. It helped those who might be allergic to certain foods, and it gave me yet another excuse to make little things with supplies from the scrapbook store.

Even a birthday party can range from simple to sumptuous. The simple menu is ordering bakery treats and making a batch of brownies of your own. (Try the chocolate malted brownies from the spa party.) For the soup, I recommend this Web site: FrontierSoups.com, where you can find dozens of varieties of delicious soup mixes. I especially like their Wisconsin Wild Rice Soup and the San Francisco Thai. Check it out and see what appeals to you. The sumptuous way to plan the soups is to make them all from scratch yourself. That's what I did, but when I got home from the store I had a moment of panic when I unpacked all the ingredients and realized what a big job I had taken on. My suggestion to you is to order a few mixes and make just one of the soup recipes from scratch.

No dessert table is complete without chocolate, but I like fruit desserts too, so I made all kinds of things. There were cookies, cakes, a cobbler, and a cheesecake. I even made Grammy's rice pudding. (The recipe is in Chapter 6.) The freezer is your friend when planning a big event like this. I made cookies three weeks ahead. I made the cakes two weeks ahead and froze those too. I wrapped everything twice in plastic wrap and then in foil for protection against freezer burn. I also made sure to label everything so my boys didn't taste anything ahead of time!

If you are stuck for ideas on sweet things, try going to the library and looking through the cookbooks. That can save you from having to buy a specialty cookbook for just one occasion. Of course, you can go online to find hundreds of ideas and recipes. I just like the feel of a book in my hands.

Here's one of the chocolate desserts I served. I made it two weeks ahead, and it freezes well.

Chocolate Pound Cake
  1½ cups butter
  3 cups sugar
  2 tsp. vanilla
  5 eggs
  1 cup unsweetened cocoa powder

2 cups flour

½ tsp. baking powder

½ tsp. salt

1 cup buttermilk

¼ cup water

In a large mixing bowl, cream butter and sugar. Beat for 5 minutes at high speed. Add vanilla. Add eggs one at a time, beating after each addition. In separate bowl, combine dry ingredients. Add dry ingredients alternating with buttermilk and water and ending with dry. Mix until well blended. Pour into greased and floured 10" tube pan. Bake at 325° 60 to 75 minutes or until toothpick tester comes out clean. Let cake cool in pan for 20 minutes. Remove from pan and cool thoroughly before serving.

Crème de Colorado Cookbook, The Junior League of Denver, Inc. (1987, 1992). Used by permission.

This party had the potential for a mountain of leftovers, so I had disposable containers ready and asked guests to take a few servings home of whatever they wanted. Instant party favor!

Since friends from all parts of my life—writer friends, church buddies, the moms in the hood, and friends from school and work—were coming, I decided nametags were a must. Some folks are shy about asking names and others have trouble remembering them. So I gave everyone a break and labeled them all.

I had invited all the women I love for so many different reasons. As the RSVPs came in I thought of how wonderful it was going to be to have each one of them there for my party. I realized I wanted to tell each woman how special she was to me, and I also knew that would be impossible on the night of the party. So with each RSVP I sat down and wrote a note on a pretty card to the guest who had just called. On the day of the party I hung long ribbons in the entry hall and clipped each note (in alphabetical order). It was a neat decoration as the guests arrived. Then when a guest was leaving I gave her the note. She had helped make my evening unforgettable, and I wanted to let her know how much she meant to me.

I wanted to give each guest a party favor; however, with 35 guests I had to think of something very small. I ended up buying some tiny boxes of unusual mints, and to make them special, I put each one in an origami box. Was it crazy to fold 35 boxes? Maybe. I found it meditative to fold. And the display of boxes waiting for the guests made a lovely decoration. You can find the instructions for folding in *The New Origami* by Steve and Megume Biddle.

The other party favor I offered my friends was a cookbook of recipes. You know how women are;

if we taste something we love, we want the recipe. I put together all the soup and dessert recipes and copied them. It was a unique remembrance of the evening, and my friends loved it. To this day, my friends tell me they are still making certain recipes from my birthday party.

I enjoyed giving this birthday party so much that I did it three years in a row. New friends joined the guest list each year. It was a blast.

The Muffin Hike

I love walking. A Sunday afternoon hike or an early morning walk—just show me the trail. Lots of my friends are hikers too. I decided it would be fun to get together for a walk. I called it the Muffin Hike. I made up a flyer and sent it out to a dozen friends.

THE MUFFIN HIKE
Meet me at Sleepy Hollow trailhead
at 8:30 Saturday morning.
We'll hike for 45 minutes and then
head back to my house for muffins.
You'll be home again by 10.
Please join me.
Let me know if you are coming,
and we'll wait at the trailhead!

This hike was a success and so easy to pull together. The simple way to have this hike is call your friends on the phone. Then pick up some muffins at the grocery store and have muffins at the trail's end when you finish hiking. Hike. Eat. Visit. Simple.

More elaborate plans for a hike with the girls include bringing each one a water bottle for the trek and having homemade muffins waiting when you all return to your house. While you're at it, cut up some seasonal fresh fruit. Set the table before you take off for the trails. Everything will be ready when you return.

And, of course, no theme is complete without variations. What if all your friends have small children? Have a stroller parade. Plan a walking route through your neighborhood, and be sure to include kid-friendly food for the big finish in your backyard. Or maybe you bike rather than hike. Plan the outdoor trek and gather those who'd enjoy cycling with you. Know your riders, and plan according to their skill level. This is not a time for competition; it's time for camaraderie. When you are selecting a spot to ride, keep in mind how folks will get their bikes there. Is this a local ride? If not, does everyone have a bike rack to use to get to the site?

I enjoyed these hikes and get togethers so much that I did them each month for nearly a year. On one of my last hikes there were only three of us; it was fun but time to call it quits. I was hiking to catch up with my friends and introduce them to each other. When Saturday mornings didn't work anymore, it was time to move on. My advice is to not lock yourself in. Enjoy what works while it's fun and when the activity has run its course, let it go. You may get to do it again sometime. Always save the good ideas!

Afternoon Tea

Afternoon tea conjures up images of little girls at tiny tables playing or big girls with hats and gloves. Either way, teatime is a lovely custom. The tradition started when Anna the Seventh Duchess of Bedford (1783-1857) realized she couldn't make it through her day from large country breakfast to late formal dinner without feeling a little "peckish" by midafternoon. So she'd ordered tea and cakes to her room at 4 o'clock, and that would see her through. It was very informal. She started inviting a few friends to join her. Soon others in her circle heard of her clever idea and the custom caught on.

These days, afternoon tea is very much a part of English culture. It can be very grand such as

High Tea featuring courses of delights. But a family spot of tea in the afternoon is still a very informal affair. It could be a part of your life too.

Tea is a pause in the day when you can have a nibble and catch up on the goings on around you. Some ladies use this as a weekly ritual to keep in touch. Mothers and grown daughters can share the news of the week. Things come up in this gentle atmosphere that never surface otherwise. People are at their ease and let their guard down. What a pleasant way to connect and share an observation or insight. No pressure.

You may think of tea as a Ritz Carlton affair, but it is really just an afternoon pause to regroup. Keep your expectations low key. Put the kettle on, clear off the kitchen table, or walk out on your patio and treat yourself to a calming cup. Once you feel the restorative powers, you'll want to invite a friend over for afternoon tea. Ask someone to join you in the garden or on the front porch. It can be a neighbor you want to know better, a friend across town you want to keep in touch with, or just the girls getting together. Coffee is for chitchat, but tea is for conversation.

Of course, if you desire to try High Tea, by all means give it a whirl. There is a great Web site that tells you all you need to know: soyouwanna.com/

site/syws/hightea/hightea.html. From obtaining
the right equipment to selecting the proper teas
and goodies, this site walks you through each step.

Here's a tea cake trick: try baking a quick
bread—banana or zucchini—in soup cans so the
bread can be sliced in cute little rounds, the perfect tea cake size. Fill the can ⅔ full and shorten
your baking time. You'll have to watch the first
batch so you can gauge the correct amount of
cooking time. Use the toothpick test.

House Cooling

My family was packing up and moving once
again. We were sad about leaving our friends but
excited about our new adventure. I have moved
every five years or so throughout my life. It seems
I'm in one place just long enough to set down
some really good roots and make good friends and
then, for a variety of reasons, it's time to move on.
We were about to move from southern to northern
California. I wanted to mark this event somehow,
not just drive off into the sunset and promise to
write and visit sometime.

If we have a housewarming when we move in,
how about a house *cooling* when we move out?
The best part is that we don't have to clean house
to get ready! There will be boxes in the way, but so

what? Use paper plates and get all the food from the deli. It's a no-fuss good-bye.

When I had a house cooling, the whole reason was to see our friends, say good-bye, and enjoy one last party together. It turned out to be a real eye opener for me. As you can probably imagine by now, I love to throw parties and fuss about the details and add all kinds of extras—all very nice but not always necessary. My only indulgence for the house cooling was the invitations. I had fun making postcards and sending them out. Then, since I was so busy orchestrating a move upstate, I couldn't plan a party with all those little things I usually like to add. And you know what? It was great fun. When I told a girlfriend I felt a little funny about the party being so casual, she jokingly suggested party favors: each guest gets to select some of your unwanted junk to take home. I wish I'd thought of it sooner, we wouldn't have moved so much stuff!

When you put your mind to it, you'll think of lots of unusual reasons to celebrate. House cooling is just one oddball idea. Are there other milestones in your life you would like to share with your friends? When Mom and Dad brought my first two-wheeler home from Sears, we had an impromptu bike parade on our block. We decorated

our bikes and ended up at my house for cookies
and lemonade. The no-fuss solution can be just as
fun as the all out extravaganza. Here's another
low-key occasion . . .

Back to School Barbecue

This school year we started what I hope will
become a tradition in our neighborhood, the Back
to School Barbecue. There are lots of kids on our
block and several of the adults work at the school.
So we are tuned in to the school calendar. I put fly-
ers in all the neighbors' mailboxes; everybody got
one even if they no longer had kiddos at home. I
planned it for the first school night of the year. We
provided the hot dogs, drinks, and dessert and
asked our neighbors to bring the side dishes such
as chips, cole slaw, fruit, whatever was easy for
them. I even asked them to bring a few extra lawn
chairs, knowing we didn't have enough for everyone. It was a pleasant evening of catching up after a
busy summer and regrouping before the fall schedule settled down around us. Most of the neighbors
were able to come—it was a school night, after all
—and they had to be home to get the kids to bed
on time. It was a simple gathering of friends to
mark something that usually passes us by.

Advent Art Show

Sometimes, though it pains me to say it, there's no food involved at all! A party without food? Sometimes an idea comes to you and you just have to act on it. The Christmas season has so many parties, it was almost nuts to add one more. But Jennie had a great idea. She had seen it once at another church and was excited for our church to try it. This is a classic case of being careful what you wish for. When Jennie suggested the idea, she was enthusiastically put in charge of the event. This meant she had more control over the outcome and could use her talents to make it happen.

Her idea was to create an art show celebrating Advent. Our congregation has many talented members, so beginning in October the call went out each Sunday from the pulpit that anyone was welcome to contribute artwork in the medium of his or her choice. Not a lot happened right away; getting a new event off the ground is tough. With the help of the church staff, Jennie identified some folks to call and ask specifically to share their talents. That got the ball rolling and the artwork started coming in. Poems, paintings, photographs, cartoons, even a baby sweater. All kinds of things came in to celebrate the coming of Christ in the Advent season.

Jennie hung the artwork and created an art gallery in the narthex of the church. Each piece was labeled with the artist's comments about the work. It was a great celebration. Each Sunday after the services there was a time to gather and look at the show. The trappings of hospitality (and good theater)—lighting, decoration, and music—came together to create a mood of celebration for Advent. It was a festival. And no hors d'oeuvres in sight.

The Road Trip

Who says you have to be at home to entertain? Take the show on the road. Think of hospitality as gathering folks who like to do the same things rather than throwing a party. That opens up the possibilities. You can go to a play, visit a museum, attend a lecture, cheer a sports team, or take in a concert. Look through the Sunday paper to find events in your area. What interests you? The opening of a new art exhibit? A play coming to town? A new restaurant? The home team on a winning streak? Use your imagination to plan an outing.

Road trips are sometimes harder to organize than having everyone to your home. There may be tickets to purchase or other details to take care of. You don't have to foot the bill for everyone, but you will need to be the instigator. Send out invitations with a very firm RSVP. Let people know you will make reservations by a certain date and that they will need to confirm they want to attend and pay for their tickets. When you have your group organized, keep things running smoothly by planning transportation. Taking the ferry to town? Carpooling? Renting a van or limo? Meeting at the event? Ease the way so your group can enjoy the event together rather than search for each other in the crowd.

Once everything is in place you can build a little excitement. If the event is weeks away, send out reminder postcards. Some silly fact about the home team you are going to see or a photo of the artwork you'll enjoy or a Web site link to the event. Be sure to include the event info again. Keep the gang looking forward to the fun to come. These little touches make it special.

Club Meetings

This doesn't mean inviting the Boy Scouts for a den meeting at your house. These are club meetings for grown ups. As with the road trip ideas, think of hospitality as gathering folks together with like interests and the possibilities surface. What kind of clubs? Book clubs, dinner clubs, movie clubs.

There are a few basics for these club gatherings. What's the purpose? It can be strictly social or for an exchange of information and learning. How often will you meet? Monthly? Every other month? Will the hostess duties rotate or will you gather just where there's room? How many in the group? Discussion groups and eating clubs do well if there isn't a crowd; eight to ten is a good number. One of your aims here is to get to know everyone well, so keep the group size manageable. The space in your living room may dictate how many people can join the fun.

Book clubs are very popular. Our local independent bookstore offers ideas of how to get started. Seek out your independent shop and explore the possibilities. A good online place to look is book-clubs-resource.com. They offer information on running a book club, reading resource guides, even book club discounts. You can organize the club for what suits you. Some clubs are structured discussion groups. Others take on a party feel with a potluck of shared appetizers. Still other groups rotate the hostess duties, each member taking a turn picking the book and planning dinner for the group. All these decisions are up to you as you create the kind of club you'd like to join.

Dinner clubs make food the feature of the evening. There are all kinds of possibilities here. You can pick a cuisine or country and have everyone bring a dish to share and the hostess makes the main course. Another fun twist is to select an ingredient and everyone has to use it in his or her dish. You can plan to cook together if your kitchen is big enough. Cooking as a group will take longer, but the shared activity can really bring people together. You can visit these two Web sites to learn more about starting your own dinner club:

entertaining.about.com/cs/dinnerparties/a/
dinnerclub.htm

everydaytraditions.com

Another good idea is a movie club. Carol was looking for something she and her husband could do together. They both love cooking, so her ideas centered on food. They were already in a book club. Carol hit on the idea of a movie club. It's less preparation than a book club because no one has to read a book to be ready for discussion.

Carol's movie club has a loose formation. Five couples get together as often as schedules allow—every month or two. The host for the evening picks a theme for the potluck—say Italian—and sets the ground rules. For example, on Italian night, no pizza, and only the host gets to make lasagna. The host also picks the movie they will watch together. Then the evening is set, dinner and a movie with good friends.

It might be time to become a Netflix member. This is an online movie rental resource: netflix .com. You create a list of movies you'd like to see. Then, for a flat monthly fee, DVDs are sent to you in the mail as the titles you selected become available. Once you are done with a film you ship it back in a prepaid envelope and they send you the next available title on your list.

Parties with a Purpose

Getting together to hang out is a great reason to invite people in, but sometimes there is more to it. Sometimes there is a financial reason involved. I'm not talking about parties where someone is selling Avon, Amway, or Tupperware. I'm talking about gatherings to further a cause or raise money for a charity, events when you bring people information as well as appetizers. Here are ideas for parties with a purpose.

Mission Trip

Churches support long-term mission trips. In many cases, though, missionaries are expected to raise money to help defray expenses. The cost of airfare, shots, living expenses, and spending money adds up quickly and can be daunting. Is there someone in your church or community who needs help reaching a financial missionary goal? Host an evening in your home where they can share their passion for their work. Show slides or a DVD or put together a scrapbook of the work they have done and would like to do. You can decorate in the style of the country where they will be and serve food from there.

When the missionary returns from the trip, you can host another event and invite the same folks who gave money and prayed for the missionary or missionary family. Your guests will love to learn how things went and see the pictures and hear the stories made possible by their donations.

It's for a Good Cause

You can entertain and give to charity at the same time. Many charitable organizations have annual fundraising events from dances to road races and luncheons to heart walks. All you need to do is pick a favorite charity and surf the Web to find out what's going on in your area.

The Susan G. Koman Association puts on the annual Race for the Cure to fight breast cancer. There are races nationwide sponsored by every local affiliate. Since the race/walk is usually early in the morning, you can have the team over to your house after the event. Or better yet, pack a tailgate party and celebrate a job well done. The simple way to do this is to have water bottles and energy bars ready at the end of the walk. Thank everyone for pitching in for a good cause. If you want to make things a little more special, spread out the blankets, pass out finger foods, and settle in for a picnic. The sumptuous way to celebrate with your team and thank them for helping out for such a worthy cause is to have a full-blown tailgater. Bring the barbecue and pull out the lawn chairs. Or have them over for brunch.

An annual event I've discovered in my area is The National Kidney Foundation of Northern California Authors' Luncheon. Six nationally known authors speak about their recent books and are available for autographs. They raise money for the Kidney Foundation and lunch is included. I have attended this event for years. I sometimes buy my ticket and encourage a friend to join me. I got ambitious one year and coaxed 10 ladies into joining me to buy a whole table. Another year, instead of throwing a birthday party for myself, I bought the whole table and invited my reader friends to join me. All the party planning was done for me because the Kidney Foundation took care of everything. We just showed up for a great day.

Sharing My Abundance

Sometimes a cause finds you. A good friend of mine had an experience that developed into a party with a purpose.

Nick was miserable with the stomach flu. Alone in his apartment, he moaned and groaned, but no one heard him. "This stinks!" he thought.

As he lay there feeling sorry for himself, it began to dawn on him that maybe he wasn't so bad off after all. *Yes,* he thought, *I'm sick and I'll be in bed for a few days, but at least I have a comfortable bed. And I can pick up the phone and have food delivered when I feel like eating. I have indoor plumbing and a clean place to be sick. There are millions in the world who do not even have a place to go to the bathroom, let alone something good to eat. There are those who feel this miserable every day. There are those who feel this bad all the time, even when they aren't sick.*

Miserable as Nick was, he knew he would get well and would not die from the stomach flu. That's when he had an epiphany. *When I get better, I'll look for a way to give back. I'll find a way to help ease the suffering of those who feel this bad all the time.*

It took weeks for Nick to find just the right idea, but he kept his eyes and ears open to possibilities. One day, he told his friend Lilly about his epiphany. He told her it was time to give something back. She agreed, and an idea was born. *What if we had a party? What if we got donations and had it at a really great venue and invited all the hip folks we can think of? We could do this!*

Lilly found an art studio in the city where they could hold the event. It was billed as a way to give back, a way to give money to the poor and have a little fun doing it. They got donations for everything from the food to the space, so every dime possible could go where it could do the most good. It was a great success.

They sold 100 tickets for $20 each, and about 80 folks showed up. It was *the* place to be that evening. The event confirmed Nick's conviction. "We can do something small and it can help. It swelled my heart. It was exciting." And it all came from a case of the stomach flu! The cause found Nick.

Food for Thought

- Is there a charity close to your heart? Find out how you can support your local chapter. They may have an event in place already that you want to join.

- Is there a cause waiting to find you? An organized charity? A missionary friend needing help? A cause you want to support? Let an idea take root.

- Is there a party waiting to happen at your house? If you have been short on ideas, take a look back over this chapter and see what sparks an interest for you. The short list: Spa Party, Birthday Party, Muffin Hike, Afternoon Tea, House Cooling, Back to School Barbecue, Road Trips, Club Meetings, Advent Art Show, A Party with a Purpose

- There all kinds of ways to entertain from simple to sumptuous and all kinds of reasons to gather the gang at your house. Be flexible and try something new for you.

5

The Littlest Hostess

Hospitality is a good legacy for you to leave your children. Kids do what they've grown up with. Your children notice all the things, large and small, that you put your efforts into. If you set the table for dinner every evening rather than sit down in front of the TV with plates in your laps, they will notice. If you plan a nutritious meal rather than getting fast food, they will notice. If they see you entertaining in your home, they will notice. If you insist on good manners, they will comply. Set the standard, and they will follow. Not only will your kids be welcome guests in the homes of others, they will become adept at offering hospitality because that's what they learned in their own homes.

Children gravitate to the things that interest their parents. My nephew plays bluegrass music quite well because he learned from his dad who plays in a band. You know what I mean. There's the swimming family: every kid is on the team and Mom and Dad are swimmers as well. I bet you know a camping family or a musical family or a family who reads or a family who gardens or is involved in sports. Every family member seems to be in on the act in some way. It's no surprise the children in the family are in on it. It's a way children can spend time with their parents. As adults, we eventually develop independent hobbies and interests, but it all starts at home as we watch what Mom and Dad like to do. If hospitality is a gift you are willing to share with your friends, it should certainly be a gift you want to give your family too.

First, it's important to teach your kids how to show hospitality and secondly it's important to be hospitable to your family. In chapter 3 I talked about the niceties you can do for your guests. Why not do some of those nice things for your loved ones? My husband and son notice when I use the cloth napkins or the good dishes. They notice when I make a special dessert or try a new recipe. Treating my family like guests raises the level of expectations in my home. When you are treated like company, you put on your company manners. Just as I don't have a party every day, I don't go to party lengths to please my family every day. But a surprise now and again keeps us all happy. It can be as simple as a note in the lunch box or fresh flowers on the table.

Traditions

When pondering hospitality as a legacy, think of things that come up every year. Do you always give your family a particular breakfast on Easter morning? Is the house decorated a certain way for Christmas? Do you have special birthday traditions? Do you have a special chair for the birthday boy or a hat the birthday girl gets to wear? These are the trappings of hospitality you have personalized for your family. It lets everyone know this is a time for celebration.

Your children will remember the little things you do to make holidays special. When I was growing up we had an Advent calendar my mother made. Every day in December my sister and I pinned an ornament on the felt banner and pulled a little treat out of the pocket. The year my son turned three, I realized it was time to make him an Advent banner. What a fun tradition to pass on to him.

Think of the cycle of your year. Are there traditions you treasure? Have you heard of things other folks do that you would like to try? Don't be shy about trying something new; you can put your own spin on it.

Holidays offer built-in celebrations, but every day can be special. What about those things you do on a weekly basis? On Fridays do you have pizza and movie night at your house? Do you play games and eat popcorn on Sunday nights? Maybe your kids make dinner every Tuesday. Is there a time you read aloud? Are there special rituals for after school or waking up? The rhythms of life offer many chances to spice things up and greet each other with hospitality.

I still remember Saturday lunchtime when I was little. My dad played a round of golf most Saturday mornings. If he came home with a big bag of barbecue potato chips, I knew he was celebrating a good game and he must have broken 100. It was a small thing, but it was a special little ritual. I love barbecue chips to this day; Dad was a good golfer!

The smallest thing can become a happy tradition. The year Zach was four, he was waiting to go to day camp in the summer. He pestered me daily. Finally I told him he would have to wait 48 days for camp to start. I knew he had no idea how long that really was, so I made a calendar just for him to cross off the days. I jotted down a few other things that were going on during the summer as well. He counted down all 48 days to camp. The next summer as we were planning things, he asked, "Where is the calendar?" Huh? I had only used the calendar to stop him from bugging me. But Zach wanted the calendar up so he could see all the plans for summer at once and count down to each event. The tradition has grown. Now I make a big calendar page for each month; it hangs on the wall in our kitchen. We keep track of all the events going on in our lives. My teenager doesn't count down the days to summer camp anymore, but he does keep track of when the next school vacation is coming.

Food for Thought

- What ways do you pass on the legacy of hospitality?

- What extravagant traditions do you have at your house? And what simple rituals do you practice at your house?

- What traditions are already in place that you want to pass along?

- Are there new traditions you want to start?

Use Your Good Manners

When Zach was little and learning social graces, I was always telling him to *use his good manners.* Rather than just telling him to say please and thank you, he had to pause a minute and think of what to say or do. I wanted him to realize *why* he was doing these things.

And why should we stress the use of good manners? Manners help keep societies civil. After all, we can't all be first in line every time. So we learn to let others go ahead of us. We use our good manners to acknowledge a courtesy done for us by saying a sincere thank you. And when we've been courteous, it's nice to be thanked. We take turns and think of each other because we are using our good manners.

This training starts at home. It's not automatic. Every toddler is the center of his or her own universe. The toddler's philosophy of life is *What's mine is mine and what's yours is mine too.* Children have to be taught to think of others. Once when I was bemoaning the fact that I had to repeatedly ask Zach to use his good manners, my friend, who runs a day care, told me her theory: "You have to say it 2,000 times for it to sink in. I'd say you are at the 1,200 mark." Ugh! Nonetheless, it's worth the effort. Manners help keep life pleasant and running smoothly for all of us.

Good manners model Christian behavior. The Golden Rule, after all, comes from the Bible. We all know it: Treat others as you would like to be treated. *Treat.* What a great choice of words. It also covers a special surprise or a tasty food. Treat others, give them something special, give them your courtesy.

Good manners extend to other situations as children grow up. At Little League and soccer practice children learn to be team players. They work together and learn to think of the team as a whole instead of just one star player. After-school play dates, scout meetings, and sleepovers are all opportunities for your son and daughter to learn to be a host. Take the time to explain to your children that when guests are in your home it's important to make them feel welcome. You can model this behavior for your kids. "Please ask your friends if they would like a snack or drink." Then your child is expected to help you serve. When they are thinking of games to play, help direct your youngster to ask what the friends would like to do first. Remind them to take turns but that the guests get to go first. It's tough to be the host sometimes.

How many times do you moan waiting for RSVPs? The courtesy of a reply to an invitation is a learned behavior. When your children get a birthday invitation, it's the perfect time to let them call to say, "Yes, I'd love to come." It's harder when they are little to say, "I'm sorry, I can't come," so wait till they're older to try that one. Still, letting them get in on the act plants those seeds. You need to treat others the way you'd like to be treated.

Remember your good manners too. When an invitation comes, you probably know right away if you can go or not. The hostess is trying to plan a fun event; she needs to know how many folks to cook for, set the table for, find seats for, and make party favors for. Be kind to the hostess.

Food for Thought

- What manners are most important to you? Are you modeling this behavior for your kids?

- It takes a lot of patience to instill good manners in our children; the payoff is so pleasant, keep at it.

Kindergarten Cuisine

There's excitement every Wednesday in Mrs. Hultquist's kindergarten class: it's cooking day. Each school year Mrs. Hultquist cooks from A to Z. She has 26 winning recipes from C is for carrot cupcakes and I is for iron sandwich to K is for (fruit) kabobs. The cooking assignment corresponds to the letter of the week. Rather than bring donuts as a treat for D week, the kids grab an apron and make "dirty dessert in a Dixie cup." Cooking is a favorite part of their week.

Simple step-by-step directions are written on large sheets of paper so the whole group can see at once. The children practice reading, measuring, and following directions. Some kids have never cooked at home, so this is s real adventure. In fact, cracking an egg is such a prized responsibility that Mrs. Hultquist has to keep track of whose turn it is to do the honors.

Cooking with kindergarteners is quite a production. They are at once timid and then rushing ahead to try things on their own. Mrs. Hultquist patiently leads them through this exciting and messy activity. People sometimes ask her, "Isn't it hard to cook with such little bakers?" She just smiles. Sure, it's a challenge some days, but the benefits are great. Sure, cooking integrates with the curriculum, but the satisfaction on their faces as they mix a cake and watch it rise in the oven is immeasurable. Mrs. Hultquist knows this is a lesson with a lifelong impact.

Little chefs take pride in their work. As accomplished chefs, we may forget to teach the little ones.

Busy cooks may be impatient with the fumbling efforts of tiny helpers. But think of the full measure of patience God has for each of us. Surely, we can offer a small amount of patience for His youngest.

Dear Father, fill me with a full measure of the patience it will take for me to pass the legacy of hospitality on to the little bakers in my life. Show me the joy of their discovery and let me join the fun. Amen.

Carrot Cupcakes
   2 cups flour
   2 cups sugar
   1 tsp. baking powder
   1 tsp. baking soda
   1 tsp. cinnamon
   3 cups shredded carrots
   1 cup oil
   4 eggs

Combine all the ingredients and beat with a mixer. Fill cupcake tins. Bake at 350° for 30 to 35 minutes.

Dirty Dessert in a Dixie Cup
   1. Make chocolate instant pudding.
   2. Crush chocolate chip cookies in a bag.
   3. Put a spoonful of pudding into a Dixie cup.
   4. Sprinkle crushed cookies on top.
   5. Add a candy gummy worm.
   6. Eat with a spoon.

Iron Sandwich

1. Butter 1 slice of bread.
2. Cut the bread into 2 triangles.
3. Take a slice of cheese and cut it into 2 triangles.
4. Place the cheese triangles on the bread.
5. Put the sandwich together.
6. Wrap the sandwich in foil.
7. Iron the sandwich by pressing firmly down and counting to 50 for each side.

Kabobs

First choose 2 or 3 fruits you would like to try.

If you choose 2 fruits, take 3 pieces of each.

If you choose 3 fruits, take 2 pieces of each.

Next, arrange the fruit in a pattern.

If you chose 2 fruits, make an "ABABAB" pattern on your skewer.

If you chose 3 fruits, make an "ABCABC" pattern on your skewer.

Who Will Come and Play?

If you delight in children and you don't have any at your house, don't despair. Go find some! Volunteer at school or church or ask the neighborhood kids to come in. If there is a kitchen available, you can try cooking with the little chefs. Use a recipe from Mrs. Hultquist's kindergarten cui-

sine or no-cook recipes. Find a children's cookbook to suits your needs. Try one of these:

*Kitchen for Kids: 100 Amazing Recipes Your
Children Can Really Make* by Jennifer Lowe. "No
youngster should pass through childhood without
making a loaf of bread or a pan of cake." I like her
thinking.

*Kids in the Kitchen: 100 Delicious, Fun &
Healthy Recipes to Cook & Bake* by Micah Pulleyn
and Sarah Bracken.

Not every church or school is set up for cooking. Pass on the gift of hospitality creatively. Do a
lesson on serving. Teach the kids the art of setting
a table. Then practice using good manners.

"Please pass the graham crackers."

"Thank you very much."

"Would you like some more?"

Or try a lesson about planning a party. Kids
are always good at telling you about their birthday
parties. Let them tell you about their latest birthday party. Ask what they planned. Ask how they
made their guests happy at the party. Of course,
they may just give you a list of the presents they
received, but it's a start. It's a good way to engage
kids in thinking about hospitality.

Food for Thought

- Do you have the patience to help a little cook learn in the kitchen? How can you do this?

- If there are no kids at your house, where could you go to help pass along the legacy of hospitality? What would it look like?

- Is it possible to volunteer at the local elementary school or your church? Check it out.

- Could you try having the neighborhood children in for a tea party or to bake cookies?

For Our Sons

There are many things every child needs to learn as he or she grows up. Cooking is one of those things. Mom will not always be around to provide meals. Knowing the basics in the kitchen is important. As my son was growing up, I let him help often. Honestly, it was a great big time waster when he was little. Once he gave up his afternoon nap, I suddenly had many more hours in the day to fill. Baking a batch of cookies with a toddler takes a long time. Fine by me, we've got all afternoon. What started as a survival technique on my part had unexpected dividends.

Zach grew up enjoying the kitchen. He also grew up eating out. He learned early to try new things and enjoy treats beyond the dessert tray. One of his favorites is a barbecued mussel. These days, when my cooking magazine arrives, he's likely to look through it for recipes he wants us to try. Some of his selections are beyond his expertise, but together we give them a try. He eggs me on to try new things.

Knowing Zach was interested in cooking, I found a cooking camp for him one summer. He and his cousin, Max, took the class together. They made all kinds of things. They roasted beef, poached salmon, fried eggplant, learned to make pasta casseroles and French bread. It was amazing. When I picked them up after class, they would be feasting on their morning lesson. They were very proud of their accomplishments. That class demystified cooking for them. Following a recipe and learning different techniques gave their confidence in the kitchen a real boost. I know that when Zach leaves home one day, he will eat well. He'll know how to provide good meals for himself and any roommates who share his kitchen.

If you have sons, teach them to cook as well as

your daughters. Carol shared these thoughts about her grown son: "A.G. discovered a man who cooked was sought after by the ladies; a girl loves it when her boyfriend bakes her a cake. A.G. makes a great chocolate cake." When A.G. left home, he took his valuable skills with him. He became a guest in demand; his hostess gift was a gourmet dessert instead of a bunch of flowers. When he was an overnight guest, he was the first one up and had the eggs benedict started! As he was growing up, the first one out of bed in the morning started the hollandaise sauce.

Eggs Benedict with Easy Hollandaise
Poached eggs
Sliced ham or Canadian bacon
Hollandaise sauce
Toasted English muffins (or try croissants)

Hollandaise Sauce
1 cube cold butter
2 egg yolks
Juice of 1 lemon (about 2 Tbsp.)
Dash cayenne pepper

Add butter, yolks, and lemon juice to a small saucepan over low heat. Stir constantly with wooden spoon. It will thicken gradually. It holds well off the heat. If sauce should separate, add 1 Tbsp. hot water and whisk rapidly to smooth out. Refrigerate any leftover sauce. Refresh later by submerging sealed container in warm water for 10 minutes then stir to blend.

To assemble and serve: Toast the English muffins. Top each half muffin with warmed ham and a poached egg. Spoon 1 Tbsp. Hollandaise sauce over top and sprinkle with a dash of cayenne pepper. Serve with extra sauce.

Carol instilled in her son a love of food, its preparation, and its presentation. It was an interest that mother and son shared. While dining out once, they enjoyed a pasta dish so much they dissected what was in it and how to make it. A.G. had a new dish to add to his repertoire.

If food is one of your passions, share it with your children. When your kids move out of the house, give them a collection of favorite family recipes. You could go crazy at the scrapbook store, but a binder of recipe card copies will be enough to get them started and keep them well-fed.

Food for Thought

- Do you think of hospitality as a female trait? Have you missed opportunities to share your gift with your son, nephew, grandson, or neighbor?

- It's never too late. Next time you need a gift idea for a graduating senior, give him or her a cooking lesson.

- Try making cooking a family affair. On the weekend get everyone in on the act and cook dinner together. Watching Dad help too is a great model for kids. The first time we cooked as a family my son was surprised my husband could cook!

6

Grandma Know-How

There was a time when ladies donned heels and an apron, sweater sets and pearls, when working in the kitchen. Not these days. When we show up in the kitchen it's to get the job done quickly and efficiently, no glamour. Some of the niceties, like fine china, cloth napkins, and slow-roasted foods have gone by the way, but the core reasons we bustle in the kitchen and make things special for our guests still remain. We love to share our homes, friendship, and faith with our families and communities.

The stories and recipes in this chapter come from the grandmas in my life. It seems the home arts come under attack sometimes these days, but entertaining and being a good hostess are timeless qualities. This chapter is a collection of gentle reminders with wisdom from the past. A pleasant gathering at home never goes out of style.

You will find these women do not skimp on real milk, butter, and sugar. These are recipes from a time when we didn't think twice about cholesterol or waistlines. There are lessons here. Don't let the calories deter you.

Jell-O

Lime Jell-O with mandarin orange slices. Orange Jell-O with carrots. Cherry Jell-O with bananas. Do you laugh at Jell-O recipes? I do. I tried one as a joke once: 12 Layer Jell-O Rainbow Salad. It took hours: make each flavor, let it set, and add the next layer. Who eats this stuff? It's so old-fashioned—grandma food. Food goes in and out of vogue.

Things change all the time. Skirts go up and down. Cars get bigger and faster. Musical tastes change. Educational ideas come and go. Political parties shift. Parenting ideas change from generation to generation. The world is in a constant state of motion. And we flow with the ideas and norms of our culture.

Technology puts a fast forward on these changes. Many shifts are a good thing. Laundry, for example, is no longer a daylong event. We can put a load in the machine and walk away. Childhood diseases are disappearing. Children get vaccines instead of serious illnesses. However, every once-in-awhile, something is lost. Some of our social graces are rusty or missing. This is a change I mourn.

I've spent pages giving you ideas for entertaining in your home. I've suggested relaxing and letting it flow and keeping your stress level low. I advised taking all the modern steps available to make hospitality work for you. But I would like to mention the social graces and suggest that Grandma had the right idea. Hospitality is one place we are losing ground to the modern way of doing things, and it's a shame.

We don't call on each other the way we used to. We don't stop by unannounced. We don't take a cake to the new neighbor. We don't use our courtesy on the road and in the store. We interrupt each other with cell phones. Or we don't call, we e-mail. We should remember to use our good manners! Be old-fashioned. Think of the other guy.

You may think I'm looking back through rose-colored glasses. But couldn't we try a little harder? There's no need to apologize for offering old-fashioned, neighborly kindness. It makes the friend feel heard, loved, and honored rather than passed over, seen through, and looked down upon.

Practicing hospitality may seem old-fashioned, something that has gone the way of high heels and panty hose for everyday use. But those niceties of calling on a neighbor and having guests in your home are still pleasant things to do. We all love to be on the receiving end, don't we? So why not be the one who makes the first move? Offer hospitality to your neighbors. Try some kindness with your coworkers. See what happens when you use the good dishes for a family dinner on Tuesday night. Your world will be a little nicer.

Planning to be a hostess is a good thing. Grandma had the right idea. So pass the Jell-O, I'll give it another try.

Food for Thought

- What old-fashioned social custom do you miss? How would it feel to give it a try again?

- Practice courtesy. Good manners are for everyone.

12 Layer Jell-O Salad

Large size packages of Jell-O in these flavors: blackberry, cherry, orange, lemon, lime, strawberry (Use any flavors you'd like to make your rainbow)
8 oz. sour cream

Dissolve 1 package Jell-O with 1 cup water. To ⅓ cup sour cream, add ½ cup Jell-O mixture. Pour this Jell-O and sour cream mixture in a 9 x 13 inch glass pan. Chill 20 minutes, making sure pan is level.

To remaining Jell-O, add 3 tablespoons cold

water and pour over chilled and firm cream mixture. Chill 20 minutes. Repeat 5 more times alternating cloudy cream mixture with clear Jell-O mixture. It takes 4 to 5 hours. Set your timer and spend the afternoon at home.

I love you this much . . .

Hamloaf was a staple at my father's house when he was growing up. We could count on having it at Grandma Peg's house when we went visiting. She always made Dad's favorites when he came home. Hamloaf is really quite good. It's like meatloaf dressed up in its Sunday best.

In 1976, my dad had brain surgery to remove a tumor. It was not successful. It would be several months before the cancer took his life, so it was time to start saying good-bye.

My grandparents planned a visit. It was a trip charged with the knowledge this was the last time they would see their son. Grandma Peg made a hamloaf, froze it, and wrapped it for travel.

At airport security Grandma Peg was asked about her foiled wrapped bundle. (This was years before 9-11.)

"It's a hamloaf for my son."

"Would you please unwrap it?"

"No."

"Ma'am, I'm going to have to ask you to un-wrap this package."

"No."

"Ma'am, please."

"No, it will spoil."

"If you refuse to unwrap this I can't let you take it on the plane."

"I am getting on the plane with my hamloaf."

"Okay, Ma'am, will you please follow me?"

Grandma Peg was led away to a small office where more security personnel tried to convince her to give up the hamloaf. Finally, in desperation, they asked her what was so important about a hamloaf. "My son has a brain tumor, and this is one of his favorite meals. I am taking it to him." Eventually, after complete X-rays of the suspicious bundle, Grandma Peg was escorted to the plane. She arrived that evening to serve her son hamloaf for dinner.

Parental love is like a force of nature, strong enough to blow objections away, gentle enough to breeze in with comfort food. Grandma Peg was a mother comforting her son in the best way she could. God comforts us in the same way. He offers peace and love a grieving mother can't match— even with hamloaf. Our earthly parents model only a fraction of what our heavenly Father can do.

God is the parent who loved us so much he came from heaven to earth to rescue us.

"Though the mountains be shaken and the hills be removed, yet my unfailing love for you will not be shaken nor my covenant of peace be removed," says the LORD, who has compassion on you (Isa. 54:10).

Food for Thought

- Can you remember a time you felt God's powerful love in your life?

- Is this a story you could share with guests in your home?

- The act of loving others may be as simple as offering them comfort food.

Hamloaf

2 lbs. ground meat (¾ ground ham and ¼ lean ground pork)
¾ to 1 cup finely crushed saltines crackers
1 can tomato soup
1 egg
⅓ cup milk
1 tsp. onion powder
pepper to taste

Thoroughly combine all ingredients and place in a loaf pan, patting down with a fork. Bake at 350°

uncovered for about 1 hour 20 minutes. Check after an hour, and if the edges are browning, cover the loaf lightly with foil for the remaining bake time. Hamloaf may need to be drained during baking if too much grease rises to the top (lean meat is essential). Let the loaf cool for 15 minutes before slicing.

The Real Deal

My husband's Grandma Whit made fudge every Christmas. She mailed it in early December so we could indulge all month. I enjoyed this delicious tradition for many years until Whit moved to a nursing home and could no longer make and mail her fudge.

At Whit's memorial service, each grandchild was asked to speak. There were many happy tears and lovely memories of this 93-year-old. When it was my husband's turn, he began by telling us, "She was a real grandma, a cool grandma. Whit wore tennis shoes and blue jeans. Whit made cookies for everyone on the block. And Whit's fudge," he began to read the recipe, "Two full sticks of butter, not margarine. Four and a half cups of sugar. This was the real deal." He passed out the recipe to everyone at the service.

The real deal. You know just by looking at the recipe this fudge means business.

The real deal. I wonder, can someone tell, just

by looking at my life, that I am a real-deal Christian? I'm afraid I do not always measure up.

The recipe calls for two sticks of butter, and I substitute margarine. Add four and a half cups of sugar, and I skimp on full measures. Melt semisweet chocolate, and I use an inexpensive brand. One teaspoon vanilla, and I sometimes forget it entirely. The results are tasteless.

I don't always follow what God asks of me. I substitute cash for service, skimp on prayer and study, and I forget to reach out in love. The results are lifeless.

The real deal is demanding. Giving God a full measure of my best means sacrifice and stretching beyond myself to serve, love, and obey. The results though, are a sweet life lived with Christ at the center.

Be imitators of God, therefore, as dearly loved children and live a life of love, just as Christ loved us and gave himself up for us as a fragrant offering and sacrifice of God (Eph. 5:1-2).

Food for Thought

- Are you substituting? How are you holding back?

- What things do you need to turn over to Christ?

- Is it too much of a stretch to practice hospitality? Why?

- How can you be the real deal?

Whit's Fudge

Combine in a large bowl:

7 oz. jar of marshmallow crème

3 12 oz. packages semisweet chocolate chips

2 cups chopped nuts

1 tsp. vanilla

1 cup butter (NOT melted)

Combine in a saucepan:

12 oz. can evaporated milk

4½ cups sugar

Bring the ingredients in the saucepan to a boil and boil gently for 8 minutes. Pour this mixture over the bowl of other ingredients. Stir until thoroughly mixed and the chocolate is melted. Pour into two 9 x 13 buttered pans. Let stand overnight to harden. Cut into bite-size pieces. Give some to all your neighbors and every grandchild.

Leave a Fingerprint

The faded recipe card reads "Emma's Gingersnaps." Emma was a friend of my Grammy Mabel. I met her when I was a little girl. She knew all about me because Grammy and Emma both bragged a lot about their grandkids. I don't really remember Emma anymore, and it makes me a little sad. But I have her gingersnaps.

I smiled today when I pulled out the ingredients to make Emma's cookies. I may not remember Emma's face, but I have a spicy smell, a cold glass of milk, and a plate of fresh gingersnaps. Emma left her imprint on me.

We touch each other countless times and in countless ways, leaving our fingerprints on the lives of others. Some impressions are deep and lasting; the big influences are easy to spot. But daily caresses sometimes go unnoticed. Help a neighbor. Be polite to a waiter. Call a friend. Donate to a charity. Be a courteous driver. All those are little fingerprints we press into each other lives.

Emma's life just brushed mine, but I received the sweet pleasure of making delicious cookies for my family. She certainly didn't imagine me baking her cookies 40 years later. Emma gave me a taste of joy. Now I pass the taste to you, brushing your life with mine, leaving a fingerprint.

Dear Father, may the fingerprints we leave in

the lives around us be made with helpful hands and a loving touch. Amen.

Food for Thought

- What imprints have you made in your day already?

- Who's left a mark on you? Remember a pleasant touch.

- Impressions you make on others may last a lifetime, so be gentle.

Emma's Gingersnaps
1 cup dark molasses
1 cup sugar
¼ cup butter
¾ cup Crisco
1 egg
3½ cup flour
2 tsp. soda
1 tsp. cinnamon
1 tsp. nutmeg
1 tsp. ginger
⅛ tsp. salt
½ tsp. ground cloves

Combine wet ingredients, then add the dry. Chill a few hours or overnight so the dough will be firm enough to work with. Roll into balls. Dip in sugar.

Bake at 350° for 10 to 12 minutes. These cookies don't spread very much so you can place them close together on the sheet.

Soaking It Up

Grammy Mabel's Sweet Rice takes patience to produce. Getting all those little grains of rice to absorb five cups of liquid takes a long time. Start slow. Heat gently. Add more.

As I stood stirring a batch of rice, I thought, *I am like a little grain of rice trying to soak up all I can. Sometimes I immerse myself in prayer or Bible study or service or praise. I try to absorb all God is offering me. When I think I am full, I discover God adds more. He reveals more of himself. Like the tiny grains of Grammy's rice, I try to puff up to full capacity.*

Making sweet rice requires a hot pot. Sometimes in our journey to know more of God, we are refined by fire. We are corrected and disciplined. The heating process is not one I like. Sometimes the lessons we learn about God are hard-won. There is pain in the journey. However, staying close to God as we go helps ease our burden. We may lose our way in the pain and drift from God. Yet God always welcomes us back with His open arms. He never left us; we are the ones that left Him.

Sweet rice takes many additions to the pot: water, milk, sugar. It's a process. Discovering more and more about God is a cycle of additions as well. It may feel like you are on a treadmill with God just out of reach. But each revelation does not have to create a frustrating cycle. Instead, it can be a delicious surprise to see more and more of God's grace, love, guidance, and forgiveness, His very essence.

Dear Father, add to my life a glimpse of your presence today. Let my journey through this day include a taste of your love and grace. I hunger to know you more and more each day. Amen.

Food for Thought

- Are you in a time of filling up? How are you seeking as much knowledge and experience of God as you can?

- If now is a time you are straying, how can you return to God?

- Are you in a time of refinement? Is the fire getting hot? How can you stay close to God so you can learn all He has to offer?

- We will never be full. There will always be more for God to reveal to us.

Grammy Mabel's Sweet Rice

    4 cups hot water
    1 tsp. salt
    1 cup long grain rice (not the instant kind)
    4 cups milk (1 quart)
    1 cup sugar
    3 eggs
    1 cup half and half
    ¼ cup butter

Bring the water to a boil, then add salt and rice.
Bring to a boil again and simmer for half an hour
until all the water is absorbed. Stir often. Add milk
and sugar. Bring to a boil and stir constantly until
the milk is absorbed, about half an hour. Beat eggs
and half and half together and pour into rice mixture and stir. Remove from heat and add butter.
Serve warm or cold. Sprinkle each serving with cinnamon sugar.

One Size Does Not Fit All

It has to taste right. The taste of your mom's
spaghetti or your dad's burgers on the grill, grandma's crumb cake, Aunt Sally's pecan pie, Uncle
George's baked beans. Tastes of home or happy
times. You want it to taste just as you remember it.

For me, one of those great tastes is sugar cookies. They come in a wide variety, from soft and
flaky to hard and crispy, and I like several different
kinds. However, the ones I crave are Mickelson

sugar cookies, soft and puffy. My Grandma Peg made these often. She passed the recipe along to my mom when she married into the family. Sometimes Mom had to fight with the dough; it can be sticky and difficult to roll out. I have the recipe now, and some batches do try my patience, but they taste so good I'm willing to wrestle.

I love these cookies, and they are *the* way sugar cookies should taste. You may love the way you make your sugar cookies—the lovely crispy kind with glazed frosting and intricate designs. But they aren't for me. I like mine better. But if I can't even give your cookies a try, what am I missing? Besides all those calories, a new way of thinking and looking at confections. When we think one size fits all, we miss out on the variety that is the spice of life.

I don't have *the* sugar cookie recipe; I have one I like very much. I don't have *the* way to show hospitality, I have a way I enjoy. I like to entertain very much, and I hope you try some of what I have to offer, but you are a unique hostess and have something to share only you can create.

We may want life to go a certain way and turn out the way we've planned. But not all of us have the same pictures in our heads. We each have an opinion of how we think things *should* turn out. If things are not going according to our plan, it's discouraging. I want my sugar cookies soft and flaky with vanilla frosting. What happens when I'm served hard and crispy or when I see burnt edges and no sweet frosting? I'll tell you what happens. I yearn for the familiar soft layers. I am convinced the other way is all wrong. Being stubborn will not help at all. I have shown you some ideas about using hospitality, now it's up to you to use what you want and then add your personal stamp to all the rest.

We all have different ways of looking at life. Free will and choice let us all chase our own dreams. God has big dreams for each one of us. And there are many ways of heading in the same direction. Share your faith when you can, hang out with your friends, and enjoy each gathering.

Food for Thought

- Do you see hospitality in one dimension? Do you think one size fits all? Why or why not?

- How can you use new insights to expand your ideas of entertaining to share your home, faith, and friendship with others?

Mickelson Sugar Cookies

⅓ cup butter
⅓ cup shortening
¾ cup sugar
1 egg
2 tsp. vanilla
2 cup flour
½ tsp. baking soda
½ tsp. salt
1 tsp. baking powder
½ cup sour cream

Mix together butter, shortening, and sugar until smooth. Add egg and vanilla. Sift together the dry ingredients and then add to the butter mixture alternating with the sour cream. Chill the dough for several hours or overnight. Roll out the dough to ¼ inch and then cut with your favorite cookie cutters. Place on greased cookie sheet. Bake at 375° for 10 to 12 minutes or until the edges of the cookie just begin to turn golden brown. Cool on a wire rack and decorate with frosting and sprinkles.

7

Beyond Your Backyard

Hospitality isn't contained within the walls of your home. Hospitality on the road can be as informal and individual as taking cookies to work or as structured as volunteering weekly at a soup kitchen. You can take meals to those in need, contribute to the local food bank, or support world hunger relief. That's hospitality in action *beyond* your home. You can take it a little further and make a conscious effort to add a few of the hostess touches on the road that you would add if you were being the hostess in your own home.

Most of my ideas for hospitality on the road revolve around food, from college care packages to contributing to the local or church food bank. How is this hospitality? Well, guests want to be fed. While our ultimate goal is to feed the heart, it's hard to listen with a rumbling tummy. So, as we meet basic needs, matters of the heart will follow. A shared table often creates a happy connection and an opportunity to share your faith.

Programs are probably already in place in your

church and community where you can become involved. Some of my ideas for hospitality on the road will have you nodding in agreement and may be things you already do. Other ideas may spark a desire to try something new. Remember, little ideas have big impacts, and what you do with a small amount of time may leave a lasting impression. When taking hospitality on the road, start small and see what develops.

Ten Minutes Can Count

What shall I compare the kingdom of God to?
It is like yeast that a woman took and mixed into a
large amount of flour until it worked all through
the dough (Luke 13:20-21).

During World War II, troop trains crisscrossed the United States. Six million soldiers and sailors passed through North Platte, Nebraska, on their way to war. North Platte was a farming community of 12,000, a ten-minute stop for the steam trains to take on water and fuel. In those ten minutes, volunteers from North Platte and neighboring farm communities offered the troops free homemade goodies: candies, cakes, popcorn balls, apples, sandwiches, milk, and hard-boiled eggs. Many of the men who returned from the war, having seen

the world and all the wonders and horrors it offered, told how that brief outpouring of affection
left a deeper impression than anything else in the
war.

When I heard this incredible story, two things
struck me. First, love and kindness sincerely offered makes a deep and lasting impression. It will
grow and multiple. And secondly, ten minutes can
count. Volunteers in North Platte had so little time
to offer their gift. But those ten minutes left a lifelong impression.

Some days I despair because I am so small in
this big world. I want to leave my mark. This story
gives me some peace and perspective. Ten minutes count. The little acts of hospitality we offer
those passing through our lives can stay with them
forever.

The Baker

I have been a proponent of Weight Watchers
for years. Weight Watchers helped me change my
eating habits as I became aware of just how many
sweets I ate. I still love desserts, and I have not giv-
en up baking. I have found a few low-fat sweets to
make, but nothing beats real butter and real sugar.

My husband and son like cookies and enjoy
having a full cookie jar. The trouble for me is that a

full cookie jar can lead to a full figure. The boys never seemed to eat as many of the cookies as I did. So I learned to make a treat when the craving hits, enjoy a serving with my family, save some for the boys, and take the rest to work. This is a great way for me to try out new recipes too. And then there are the times I see a recipe that sounds scrumptious to me, but I know my family won't touch it. I can play in the kitchen and share the results with my coworkers.

I didn't realize how much of a habit this had become until one Monday morning I overheard someone in the staff room say, "Bummer, Lisa didn't bring in anything today." I'm known as the baker. I am often asked why I bake so much; usually I just say I had a craving. But sometimes I take a chance and say, "I wanted to do it because I care about you, and it's a way to serve." What started as feeding my own craving has turned into a pleasant routine for giving to others. At least once a month, I see to it that something from my kitchen shows up in our staff room.

Here's a recipe that travels well and is very popular with my coworkers. It's even low fat.

Spice Cake
1½ cup flour
¾ cup packed light brown sugar

1 tsp. baking soda

½ tsp. baking powder

1 tsp. cinnamon

½ tsp. ginger

¼ tsp. nutmeg

¼ tsp. cloves

½ tsp. salt

¾ cup fat free sour cream

2 Tbsp. vegetable oil

1 cup applesauce

Preheat oven to 350°. Coat a 9" square pan with cooking spray. Stir together in a large bowl the flour, sugar, baking soda, baking powder, spices, and salt. Stir together the sour cream, oil, and applesauce in a small bowl. Stir the sour cream mixture into the flour mixture just to mix. (Do not beat.) Spoon batter into prepared pan and bake until a toothpick inserted in the center comes out clean, about 45 minutes. Allow cake to cool to room temperature before cutting into 16 pieces.

Do you love to bake too? Save your figure and share the fun. Let coworkers know you care by bringing them a homemade treat. Add your own hospitality touch by putting the cookies in a lovely basket with a cloth napkin or arrange the goodies on a pretty plate. Sometimes I even bring flowers from the garden (or grocery store). I often write a little note to go with the treats.

If you don't work in an office, be creative.

Drop off treats for the staff at your child's school or the church office. Send something to work with your spouse. Think about who needs some appreciation and surprise them. Or really get serious and try the Great American Bake Sale.

The Great American Bake Sale

The Great American Bake Sale is a nationwide event that started in 2003. This event raises money to fight childhood hunger. Bake sales have always been a popular fundraising tool. The sponsors, *PARADE Magazine* and Share Our Strength, took this local idea nationwide. Any baker from child to grandma can set up a stand and help the cause.

Here's how it works. You register for free at the Web site, greatamericanbakesale.org, host a bake sale, and send the funds to Share Our Strength. It can be as simple as you and your kids making cookies and brownies all week and selling them curbside, or it can be as elaborate as involving a whole group of bakers, drumming up donations from local bakeries, and setting up your sale at a mall. The Web site is complete from labels for baked goods to answers about tax questions. There are also many success stories to read. It's easy and helpful.

If baking is one of your passions, use it in your community. Much of the money raised by The

Great American Bake Sale stays right in the local organization working hard to combat hunger in your area. The Web site will answer your questions of which businesses and organizations are involved, so even if you don't sponsor a bake sale, you can support those who do.

On the day of the bake sale, make your sales area inviting. This is your table even if it is curbside or in the parking lot of a strip mall. You can add your own touches to make even a bake sale feel like a party. Drape the table with one or more cloths; tie the baked goods with ribbons; put flowers on the table; engage your customers in conversation. This is an opportunity to share why you are doing this in the first place.

Coupon Mom

Stephanie Nelson is the Coupon Mom. You may have visited her Web site: couponmom.com or seen her on *Good Morning America* or read articles she has written for a variety of magazines. I became aware of her expertise in an article she wrote for *Guideposts* about saving money on the grocery bill by clipping coupons. Granted, it's a very old idea, but her article included ideas I'd never thought of before.

The practice I found most intriguing was using

coupons to fill the shelves at the local food bank. The idea is to use the buy one/get one free coupons and use one for your household and one for the food bank. I used to laugh at the coupon offers of 10 for $10 or 20 for $10. Who buys stuff in such mass quantities? Well, you can. Use some of what you buy for your household, and take the rest to the local food bank. Stephanie's Web site has many ways to help others; it is well worth a visit.

The Care Package

College finals. What memories I have of those long study hours, crazy stress levels, and my eagerness to get home when it was all over. Our women's ministry team remembers. Each year we collect the names and addresses of college students in our congregation, then send out care packages during finals week just after Thanksgiving. We usually send out about 50 packages. We've refined the process over the years. Originally, we sent homemade cookies in carefully wrapped and decorated shoeboxes. We discovered, however, that what the student received was a stale box of crumbs. Now we make Chex Mix and buy hard candies. We ship the goodies in coffee cans or gallon cans from the local paint store. (Some paint stores will donate the cans to your cause.)

The students have let us know how much they enjoy getting this encouragement from home. Sometimes the goodies result in good conversations with other students about faith. "Where'd ya get the Chex Mix, dude?" It's an easy opening. Wow, remote control share-your-faith. You don't even have to be there to help spark a conversation.

Chex Mix

   6 Tbsp. butter
   2 Tbsp. Worcestershire sauce
   ¾ tsp. garlic powder
   1½ tsp. seasoned salt
   ½ tsp. onion powder
   1 cup mixed nuts
   1 cup pretzels
   1 cup garlic or regular bagel chips
   3 cups Corn Chex cereal
   3 cups Rice Chex cereal
   3 cups Wheat Chex cereal

Heat oven to 250°. Melt butter in large roasting pan in oven. Stir in seasonings. Gradually stir in remaining ingredients until evenly coated. Bake 1 hour, stirring every 15 minutes. Spread on paper towels to cool. Store in an airtight container. Makes 12 cups of snack mix.

Mug & Muffin

What's more pleasant than having coffee with

a girlfriend or two that includes a sweet treat and some good conversation? Mug & Muffin get-togethers are popular at many churches. You bring the mug and we'll bring the muffins. I led this ministry for several years. It's a place for women of the congregation to form deeper connections with one another. Ours was relaxed and casual, and we met on Saturday mornings.

I always asked one of the regulars to help make muffins (or a goodie of her choice). Then I came up with a conversation starter. Unlike Sunday mornings when everyone is running around in a hurry, Saturday mornings gave us time to chat and get to know each other. Some topics we introduced to get the conversation going were books you love, movies to see, Easter traditions, love stories (how you met), and summer vacation memories. Of course, pressing concerns sometimes came up such as in-laws, joys (or trials) of grand-parenting, worries about children. Whatever the topic, it was thoroughly discussed.

Sometimes we enjoyed a short program. A pregnancy resource center sent a representative to talk to us once and raised awareness and funds. One month our new pastor's wife was the guest of honor. One December gathering we had a gift-wrap how-to seminar, and that was a huge hit.

Mug & Muffin is a ministry of hospitality you may be interested in. There doesn't have to be a church connection. Your Mug & Muffin might be a monthly gathering of neighbors or coworkers in your own home. The goal is to have a place for women to connect.

Here's a Mug & Muffin favorite:

Biscotti with Mini Chips

¼ cup sugar
2 Tbsp. butter
1 whole egg
1 egg white
¾ tsp. vanilla
¼ cup unsweetened applesauce
1½ cup flour
¼ tsp. baking powder
Pinch salt
3 Tbsp. mini-semisweet chocolate chips

Heat oven to 350°. Lightly coat a baking sheet with cooking spray. In a large bowl, mix sugar and butter until smooth. Add egg, egg white, vanilla, and applesauce. In another bowl mix flour, baking powder, salt, and minichips. Add butter mixture. Using a dough hook, mix with electric mixer on low speed until no longer sticky. (If your mixer doesn't have a dough hook, mix by hand, turn out on a floured board, and knead for 30 seconds.) Add additional flour a tablespoon at a time if necessary. Place dough on a lightly floured surface. Form into a roughly 3 x 10 inch log. Place on baking sheet and bake for 25 to 30 minutes. Remove from the oven and cool for 10 minutes. Reduce the oven to 275°. Using a serrated knife, cut the warm log crosswise on a slight diagonal into ½-inch-thick slices. Stand the slices, about an inch apart on the baking sheet and return to the oven for 12 minutes. The centers will be soft, but biscotti will crisp when cooled.

Soup's On

Feed the homeless. Get involved in the food bank. Volunteer at a soup kitchen. There are so many ways to feed those in need. In my area there is a program called Homeward Bound. For 20 years it has served meals to those in need on a weekly basis. Eight churches have banded together to keep this program going. Each church has teams that provide food for the day. They bring boxes of cereal for breakfast and make casseroles for dinner. Some team members contribute money for food instead of cooking.

Programs exist in every city to fill this urgent need. Seek one out in your area. Ask at church or your local food bank. When you volunteer, serve as you would in your own home—with your best recipes if you cook, or with your biggest smile if you are dishing up what's been donated. Make the people feel like guests.

The Lunch Bunch

Years ago, my husband, Rod, worked at a company that provided lunch for the employees every Friday. The unusual part was that the workers took turns cooking. Everyone signed up for a couple of times each year. People who didn't cook made arrangements for food to be delivered from a favorite restaurant. There was a budget for Friday lunches.

Just back from paternity leave, it was Rod's turn. Our son Zach was one month old. Rod decided his Friday would be Lunch with Zach. His theme was "school lunches." Thursday night we packed lunches. We filled 30 brown paper bags with chips, fruit, and homemade cookies. On the way to work Rod picked up deli trays, bread, condiments, and soda. Lunch turned into a nostalgic adventure. When people saw the brown bags, the first thing they did was start trading Fritos for Cheetos and apples for bananas—just like school days. Zach and I showed up for the fun too. It was a huge success.

Few companies offer free lunch every week. But "The Lunch Bunch" is a popular notion. We spend 40 hours or more each week with our co-workers. Sometimes we might want to escape at lunchtime for a quiet moment or dash off to do an

errand. But often it's nice to visit with our friends.
Two recent magazine articles reinforced this
thought.

Lisa Marie Rovito of Brooklyn, New York,
wrote to *Guideposts* (May 2006) about her group
of brown baggers. One summer they enjoyed a
daily lunch on the office-roof patio. When the
weather turned cold, rather than not eat together,
they moved to the conference room. A worker vol-
unteered to cook for the whole group one day.
Now, each Monday someone takes his or her turn
making lunch for the group, offering a family favorite or trying a new recipe. What started by
chance because of a change in the weather has
grown into a great time of sharing.

Cooking Light (March 2006) took an even
more structured look at The Lunch Bunch. Sue
Nechanicky was looking for a lunch alternative
to vending machines, eating out, or bringing a
healthy but incomplete meal from home. Sue
launched the Healthy Lunch Club at her office in
Minneapolis. Every day three members of the
club make enough food to feed 10 people. They
follow a few guidelines to make the meals healthy.
Once a member has cooked, he or she gets two
weeks off. Most lunch members spend $40 to $50
on the meal when it's their turn to provide. Do the

math; this is a substantial savings for two weeks of healthy lunches, and the sense of community is priceless.

At the school where I work we have Friday treats. Four of us at a time take turns bringing goodies to enjoy during morning recess. Some weeks it is quite a spread and spills into lunch: miniquiches, salads, dips, cookies, cakes, and fruit platters. The kids aren't the only ones looking forward to recess!

Here's a Friday treat we love . . .

Warm Artichoke Dip

    2 14 oz. cans oil packed marinated artichoke hearts
    2 10 oz. packages frozen chopped spinach, thawed and squeezed dry
    1 cup grated Romano cheese
    1 cup low-fat mayonnaise
    ½ cup light sour cream
    ½ onion chopped
    3 garlic cloves minced
    Dash of cayenne pepper
    Zest of one lemon

Drain the artichoke hearts and rinse under warm water, then chop them in a food processor. Place all the ingredients *except* the lemon zest in a large Dutch oven and mix well. Cover and cook until the cheese has melted and the dip is hot—about 30 minutes. Stir in the lemon zest. Serve the dip warm.

> Try dipping carrots and snap peas, as well as crackers.

Is a Lunch Bunch possible where you work? Mention the idea and see what the response is; you may be surprised. If it falls flat, don't be discouraged. Maybe once or twice a year you can provide lunch for the gang. You could try the simple brown-bag idea my husband and I used for Lunch with Zach. Or if there's a special time of year for you—say when the tomatoes are in full swing in your garden or Secretary's Day—bring lunch in for the office.

Every St. Patrick's Day the principal at our school provides a potato bar with all the trimmings for the staff. It's a special day to her and a tradition we look forward to. It certainly makes us feel cared for. Is there a special day for you to show your coworkers you care for them?

First Fruits

One of the things churches do well—really well—is bring food. We bring meals to new moms, recovering patients, and shut-ins. We all want to help. We all have the same good thoughts. And it seems we all bring the same meals—chicken or lasagna. But what about the recipients? How much lasagna can they graciously accept?

Bringing a meal is an opportunity for joyful service. If I show up with the same meal everyone else has provided, did I offer my best? Did I share my first fruits? Jesus said that when we gave to one of His brethren we gave to Him. He could probably eat ten pans of lasagna and not complain, but it's harder for us to put a happy face on repetition, even when it's offered in love.

I don't make very good lasagna, and buying a roasted chicken from the store seems like cheating when I've committed to bring a home-cooked meal. I bring the pocket sandwich instead. And when I make it, I make two; one for my family and one for the family I am serving. In the morning when I set out the frozen bread dough, I say a little prayer for the family. All day when I pass the rising dough, I think of the dinner I will serve. I offer my first fruits: joyful prayer and creative cuisine.

Tip: I bring this sandwich with cut-up fresh fruit, a big bag of chips, and homemade cookies or brownies. All of it keeps well and can be served warm or cold.

Pocket Sandwich
   1 lb. bulk sausage
   1 16 oz. loaf frozen bread dough, thawed
   2 cups mozzarella cheese

1 egg white slightly beaten
sesame seed
marinara sauce for dipping

Brown the sausage and drain well on paper towel.
On a lightly floured surface, roll out the thawed
bread dough into a rectangle about 15 x 8. Sprinkle
with cheese, leaving a 1 inch border around the
edge. Next, layer on the crumbled sausage. Pinch the
edges of the bread dough together and flip, seam
side down, onto a greased baking sheet. Brush with
egg white so it will brown nicely and sprinkle with
sesame seeds. Bake at 350° for 30 to 35 minutes.
Let stand for 10 minutes before cutting into slices
and serve with marinara sauce for dipping.

Be kind to the people you are serving by bringing your meal in disposable containers. If they are
receiving many meals in a row it will be difficult to
keep track of serving dishes from so many hostesses. I deliver the sandwich on a disposable cookie
tray from the grocery store. I put the fruit and
brownies in Gladware or Ziploc containers.
There's nothing to return to me.

More than Prayer

I clicked open the e-mail from my friends in
Minnesota thinking how nice it was to hear from
them. But what I read was an urgent request for
prayer. Barry had been in a serious bicycle acci-

dent and shattered his jaw and lost many of his teeth. Tears ran down my face. I knew he was not going to die from his injuries, but the trauma was great. I needed to do something. Dropping everything and flying to Minnesota was not an option. Even at this distance, I knew I could pray. But I wanted to do more; this situation called for action.

One of my prayers was, *Dear Father God, I know wrapping Barry in prayer is important, but I have a burning desire to do something more. Please calm my heart so I can be an effective prayer warrior, or show me a way to do more.* Send cards. I sent a funny one, a serious one, and a plain one. I found more. I sent another round of cards. And still more. I bridged the distance with prayer and mail for weeks. God had shown me a way to do something.

I clicked open an e-mail from church. What I read was an urgent request for prayer. Mike had put a severe gash in his leg while chopping wood. I knew he would not die from his injury, but the trauma was great. I prayed. Again, one of my prayers was for me, *Dear Father God, calm my heart and make me effective where you need me.* Make the muffins. Mike had raved about my orange muffins on several occasions. I checked my pantry; I had all the ingredients, and I had the time. I made a batch of muffins and took them to Mike's house.

Prayer during a crisis is essential, but I'm still learning to latch onto prayer as the *best* alternative. I admire people who can pray and find comfort in offering prayer alone. I can't. Happily, God gives me other outlets as well. He shows me how I can use my gift of hospitality. He knows I am not strong enough for prayers alone; He knows I need to DO something.

Listen to your heart when you ask God what you should do during a crisis in someone's life. He will show you how to use your gifts if you listen.

Orange Muffins

    1 cup sugar
    Juice of one orange
    (or ½ cup juice from concentrate)
    ½ cup butter
    1 cup sugar
    ¾ cup sour cream
    2 cups flour
    1 tsp. baking soda
    1 tsp. salt
    Grated orange rind of one orange
    ½ cup chopped nuts (optional)

Mix 1 cup sugar and orange juice. Set aside for dipping after muffins are baked. Cream together remaining butter and sugar. Add sour cream alter-

nately with the dry ingredients. Fold in orange zest
and nuts. This is a stiff batter. Use a well greased
mini-muffin tin (for bite-size muffins). Bake at 375°
for 12-15 minutes. While still warm, dip tops of
muffins in the sugar/orange juice mixture. Cool on
a wire rack. Makes about 48 mini muffins.

Someone's Gotta Make the Coffee

Years ago, I did a little civic theater. I worked
the light board for a production of *Death Trap*.
This was long before computerization. I took
down the house lights; I brought up the sun in Act
One. I created a lightening storm in Act Two. I
was unseen. As a technical understudy my name
wasn't even in the program.

I was backstage, but it was still exciting. I felt
nervous with all those switches at my command.
Then I felt powerful when I cracked the first bolt
of lightening in the electrical storm. How dramatic! I was an integral part of the production, though
the applause at the curtain call was focused on the
actors and not directed at me.

I thought recently of how I am often behind
the scenes, out of the spotlight. I am not the one
with the brand-new baby; I am the one who
shows up with a couple of meals so Mom gets
time enough for a shower. I am not the one with
the chronic illness; I am the one who sends cards,

books, and phone calls. I am not the one with the new condo; I am the one who helps move in and brings a little housewarming gift. I am not the one with the flooded home; I am the one with the shovel who shows up to help. I am not the one without winter clothes; I am the one who knits sweaters to donate. I am not the one living paycheck to paycheck; I am the one who can give money. I am not the one.

I was feeling a little blue about being backstage—we all crave the spotlight sometime—when a dear friend put my role in perspective. "You are an encourager, Lisa. You lift up those who need it for a minute." Maybe you are an encourager too.

Someone has to be behind the scenes. Someone's gotta make the coffee. Someone's gotta set up the chairs for the event. Someone is there to listen. Someone has to watch, to be aware, to see when little encouragements are needed. You show the world a piece of God's grace when you use the gift of hospitality.

When we look at service like that, we should all be waiting in the wings of the theater to support the principle players in every life around us. What a joy!

I laughed at myself for feeling small. The title of the job I get paid to do is Assistant Instructional

Aide. I am a professional aide. I should have seen the merit in my role all along. Find merit in your role as hostess whether you are at home or on the road. We offer a reflection of God to the world.

Food for Thought

- What ideas in this chapter sparked your interest?

- What other ideas come from thinking of these beginnings?

- Can you view hospitality beyond your home? What does it look like?

- How can you add the touches of hospitality you use at home when you take a meal or deliver some service to another?

- Where do you want to get involved?

- How can you investigate to see what's out there? Web search? Church bulletin? Community board?

8

Thanks for Coming

It's almost time to end our visit. This final chapter focuses on ideas to help keep you going when it gets hard to open your home or give one more person your hospitality. Here are some insights into attitude, patience, setbacks, and just being in the right place at the right time. Like the first chapter, this is a collection of devotionals and a few reminders of why to keep hospitality happening.

The Comfort Zone

"That's outside my comfort zone." Have you heard this phrase? Pushed beyond what is pleasant, easy, and familiar, we find ourselves outside our comfort zones. Breaking free of the familiar can help us grow in unexpected ways though. Sometimes we step out bravely and try a new experience and are pleasantly surprised by positive results. Sometimes we are dragged through an experience and do not see any positive gains.

This year my brother, sister, and I gave my mom a laptop for Christmas. It was the only item on Mom's wish list. My mom's only hands-on exposure to computers had been looking over my shoulder while I clicked on a Web site or sent an e-mail. So it surprised us all when she was finally ready to have a computer of her own. She was both excited and nervous.

I called Mom after New Year's to see how she was doing. "Well, I've opened the box and I've read the manual." Wow, such progress I giggled to myself. Mom was inching outside her comfort zone. The next week I phoned and found out she'd had a three-hour lesson with a very patient, computer-savvy friend. Mom was well beyond her comfort zone.

Does practicing hospitality put you outside your comfort zone? Is the thought of entertaining scary to you? Maybe you feel like my mom when she opened the box of her new computer. "I want to use this and do all the fun things I've heard it can do. But I also want to run and hide because it's a lot to learn." Well, like my mom read her computer manual, you've read a book that might help you out of your hospitality comfort zone. Figure out your next small step.

I have been thinking about our desire to stay in our comfort zones and our need to be pushed beyond them. If I stay only where I am settled and content, I become stagnant. Yet, if I am always on the edge, I never find peace. Neither extreme is acceptable. When we are out of our level of familiar and peaceful, God is out there too. Whether we step out in nervous excitement to try something foreign like my mom surfing the Web, or we feel dragged into something like trying out hospitality, God is there, right where we need Him, comforting and supporting us. Lost in a sea of technical computer jargon? Intimidated by entertaining company in your home? He will help you through these challenges. God is our comfort zone.

Now may the Lord of peace himself give you peace at all times and in every way. The Lord be with all of you (2 Thess. 3:16).

Food for Thought

- What aspects of hospitality are beyond your comfort zone?

- How can you work around these and ease into using your hospitality muscles?

Marinated with Patience

Patience. I do not have an abundant supply. I am not good at letting things simmer. I'm always wondering if it's done yet, always lifting the lid or opening the oven door to check. It's a wonder I ever marinate anything; there is too much patience involved. So to suggest a recipe that has to marinate overnight, well, it must be really tasty or a leap of faith. These ribs are good and leaving them just a few hours is perfectly fine, but the flavor mellows and is even richer if you let them marinate a whole day.

I get requests for this recipe, and I always caution the cook that there's a long list of ingredients and you have to marinate. They are usually still eager to try. Yet, I wonder if anyone ever does. We live in a time when most cooks want instant results.

Tests of my patience are not limited to the kitchen. Waiting in line, driving in rush hour traffic, phone call interruptions are all irritating to me. I am impatient in other ways as well. I get annoyed with God and His plan for my life. I don't want to wait and see, I want to know now! However, the journey always teaches me more than I learn after I arrive at my destination.

Just telling you these ribs are delicious is not enough. Giving you the recipe isn't enough. Feeding you the end result wouldn't do either. Making them on your own, that would give you satisfaction and the delight of discovery. Just telling you hospitality is a gift from God you can open and use with delight is not enough. You are going to have to find out for yourself. The journey is well worth it. I trust you have found some helpful ideas from this book. It's time to test things out.

Food for Thought

- What tests your patience? Kids? Chores? Waiting? Interruptions? Rather than pray for more patience, try being very specific with God. Take a deep breath and ask for help with one area in which you struggle.

- Are you stuck? Have you read this book on hospitality and thought that it's nice but you aren't sure it's for you? Test the gift; give it one opportunity to take root. What suggestion from these pages excites you?

Patient Pork Ribs
¾ cup soy sauce
¾ cup orange marmalade
½ cup pineapple juice
3 to 5 cloves garlic, pressed
2 Tbsp. fresh ginger, minced
3 tsp. fresh rosemary, chopped
1 Tbsp. lemon juice
1 Tbsp. sesame seeds
2 to 4 Tbsp. cooking sherry
¼ tsp. pepper
4 to 5 lbs. pork back ribs

In a large bowl, mix all the ingredients except the ribs. Rinse the ribs and pat dry. Place the ribs in a gallon-size plastic bag. Pour in the marinade and coat the ribs. Place in the refrigerator for several hours or overnight, turning a couple times. Line a pan with foil, set a rack in the pan. Lift ribs from marinade and arrange in a single layer. Pour marinade in a bowl. Bake ribs at 350° basting every 20 minutes with marinade for the first hour. Bake until ribs are browned and meat pulls easily from the bone, about 1¼ hour.

Come to the Buffet

That was delicious! I savored the last bite then laughed at myself. I am so not a salad person. Eating greens is a taste I've had to acquire. I'll tell you two little secrets: first, all greens are not created equal, and second, it doesn't take a mountain of toppings to make a salad.

I used to think of salad as half a head of iceberg lettuce, croutons, and a quarter cup of dressing. No wonder I shied away. I have discovered salad is a spring mix of greens and a whole lot of an arugula topped with two sliced strawberries, pinches of mozzarella, and just five chopped pecans. The dressing isn't drowning the salad; it's a splash of flavor for the greens to dip in rather than wade through.

I sat with the taste still lingering on my tongue

and smiled at my change of attitude. Let's face it, I only ate salad to lose weight as summer approached. Variety, adventure, and unique combinations have changed my attitude toward greens. I have shifted my perspective from deprivation to a buffet of healthy alternatives. I've unlocked choices.

What is your view of hospitality? For some it's one of "I have to." When you view it as a duty, yes, it's annoying and irritating. What can change your attitude? There are many different ways to start small and find the joy of sharing your faith through hospitality. I didn't instantly love eating my greens, but I discovered ways to make them delicious to my palette. You may not instantly be ready for a full-scale dinner party for ten, but maybe you can find ways to entertain on a small scale. What works for you? Decide what there is about hospitality that appeals to you. Pick the details you love and try them out. Read again the sections of this book that had you pausing to think, *Hey, that sounds like fun. I'd like to try that.* Unlock the choices that appeal to you.

Food for Thought

- Does your attitude need an adjustment? How can you stop moaning about how much work you think hospitality will involve and instead take a small step toward acting on your good intentions?

- Think of a time when you were blessed by a simple gathering—maybe tea with a friend. What made it special? Can you give that gift of time and hospitality to someone?

- What part of hospitality appeals to you the most? Can you put that one small piece to use? Food prep? Take some cookies to a neighbor, or in to work. Getting people together? Invite two friends over for tea some afternoon. Small steps.

Disaster Dinners

Disaster dinners. I have had my fair share. I marinated chicken in lemon for too long and it turned to rubber. I broiled rather than baked a casserole. I've undercooked, overcooked, and forgotten to cook. I've tried recipes that sounded delicious but tasted awful. I don't always get it right and dinner becomes a disaster. On those evenings we end up with a peanut butter and jelly sandwich or a bowl of cereal for dinner.

Sometimes I laugh over my dinner mistakes and we enjoy the treat of junk food for dinner. But sometimes I am too hungry and grumpy to see any humor in the situation. Nonetheless, there's always another chance to cook up something great tomorrow. A new start in a clean kitchen with fresh ingredients.

I am not too hard on myself over a messed up meal, but when I've blown it with God I want to run and hide. I'm sure there are no second chances. I can't start again. And yet God is far more forgiving then a grumpy chef. God gives me a new start, a clean life, and a fresh beginning any time and every time I need one and am ready to ask for it.

Not every time you offer someone the hospitality of your home will it turn out to be a fantastic experience. Sometimes it may turn into a disaster. Any number of things can conspire against you from food mishaps to guests getting their feelings hurt in some way. Why try again? Remind yourself that God gives you a new chance every day to bask in His glory and be given His grace. If He can be gentle with you, try to be gentle with yourself. Dust yourself off and try again another time. Plan another gathering and see what comes of the next encounter.

Food for Thought

- Have you ever had a dinner disaster? What happened?

- Was the disaster beyond your control, or was there a lesson to be learned from your mistake?

- What can you do differently next time?

- What setbacks have you had in your pursuit of hospitality? Are these enough to make you stop? Or would you consider taking a break and then trying again.

The Big Picture

As I mentioned earlier, I'm not too patient. I want to know *now*. I want to have all the information *now*. I need it! I deserve it! Sometimes I get demanding of God. I figure He needs a talking to. He needs to know how desperate I am. He's not letting me in on the big picture and it's bugging me. This is my life. Yes, I gave it over to Him, but I still want control!

Recently we ordered our son an iPod for his birthday. Zach was excited to say the least. He

waited every day for the FedEx truck to come. At
the end of the week, voila! Except the box that arrived was marked Box 1 of 2 and filled with the
software we'd also ordered. "It's never going to
come!" he moaned. With the Internet we could
find Box 2 with the click of a mouse.

We had ordered online so we could track the
package. We looked at the FedEx Web site and
found our tracking number. Then every day we
watched the progress of Zach's iPod. The route
was far different then we anticipated. For one
thing, it started in Shanghai, China! We watched it
arrive in Anchorage, Alaska. Then it took off and
flew to Indianapolis, Indiana, where it spent the
night. A day later the iPod was sent to Oakland,
California, where it spent the weekend. Bright and
early Monday morning the doorbell rang and at
9:27 A.M. I signed for the package. It was all
recorded online; we checked. It was amazing.

What does all this have to do with my being
bugged by God not letting me in on the big picture? Let me explain. FedEx handles millions of
packages every night; they all get routed just where
they are supposed to go. All the items are sorted
and shipped in the most efficient way. FedEx sees
the big picture. With a tracking number on each
box they can locate any item and tell you where it

is, but they do not give you a reason for why it is flying over California to Indiana before returning.

God doesn't give us all the reasons for His routing system either. There is no Web site for us to log on to find out where the next step in our lives is going, or for that matter, where the next important encounter is coming from. We have to trust God. There it is, the hard part: Trust God. We have to have faith, knowing He has the big picture in mind. He knows why it will take weeks (years) for a package to arrive safely on our doorstep at just the right time. He doesn't explain it. You may not see how hospitality fits into God's plan, but if it makes your heart sing and it's the job you were asked to do, go for it!

We all have free will. Factor that into the big picture and sometimes the route takes longer. We tend to mess things up for ourselves. What if I had decided that a friend in Indianapolis could go to FedEx and pick up the package and hold it for me since I'd be visiting in two days? But the big picture called for the package to go to Oakland the next day. My friend misses getting the box and off it goes to Oakland. I miss the home delivery since I'm in Indianapolis visiting. Now I delay getting the gift for a week because I stepped in, thinking I knew better. I messed it up. I still get the package;

I just made it harder on myself. I didn't trust FedEx to deliver.

I don't always trust God to deliver. I think He could solve this problem for me by just telling me what's going on! But there's that free will thing again. God is not in the business of controlling our lives; we make choices all the time and then He works within the decisions we make. How can having guests in my home make any difference to anyone? There may be so many connections, God can't tell you all the reasons. Or it could be as simple as today was the day a particular guest needed to feel loved, and God sent you to do it.

In this information age it's difficult to accept "taking it on faith," but I think it's the very thing God asks us to do. I have to check in with Him more often if I don't know what He's up to. I pray. I learn to trust Him. He always delivers, but with a routing system that makes sense to His big picture. There might be adventures in Anchorage and Indianapolis I know nothing about, maybe my package was picking up some good stuff I hadn't even ordered! I have to trust, and that is the hardest part.

We do not always get to know the outcome of our adventures in hospitality. We may fumble in the beginning, unsure of how to start. We have it in mind to share our faith by inviting people into our home. There, a simple start. A few times it may work out the way you envision: You'll be invited to share your faith on the spot. However, most times we are asked to love and care for others rather than preach to them. Sharing your faith is done by opening your life to people and then being yourself with them. And hospitality is only one way to be yourself. Someone else might open his or her life through music or sports or crafting or any number of pursuits. There are a variety of ways to show God's love to the world and plant seeds of love and faith. It's not up to us to know the outcome. It's up to God to tend the seeds of faith and love that were planted.

Dear Father, Help me trust you with this adventure in hospitality. Let the seeds I plant be enough. Take away any worries I have of needing to continually cultivate each seed. I trust you to tend the garden. Amen.

Food for Thought

- How can you turn over control of your hospitality gift to God?

- Can you take it on faith that hospitality has a purpose? What do you feel the purpose is?

Movie Meals

Wow, a real movie set! This is exciting. There's the crew setting up the camera and the actors milling around waiting to get started. There's the director busy talking to the cameraman. I'm standing in the background holding my breath. It's finally happening.

Two years ago, my husband, Rod, wrote a script. A year ago, he started scouting for a location and getting his crew together. Six months ago, he got the equipment. A month ago, he auditioned the actors. Then, he rented the truck. One recent morning, we drove to the middle of nowhere to start shooting. All this for nine minutes that will be called *Corpus Delicti*.

I wanted to help in some way, but I had nothing to do. I was just a silent cheerleader offering moral support. I came to see my husband yell, "Action!" and "Cut!" just like in the movies.

They set up the first shot, cameras roll, and a plane flew overhead. "Cut!" They try again. "Action!" The wind picks up and the actors' words fly away. "Cut!" Eventually they get the shot they want and move one. All morning they work hard. Lunchtime approaches.

Shopping bags appear and the producer pulls out deli sandwiches, bags of chips, and cans of soda.

Everyone gathers round to grab a bite of lunch. The crew is famished. As we all dig into lunch it dawns on me how I can help, "Tomorrow," I announce, "I'll bring a homemade lunch." There are smiles all around. I'm ready to make them something special. In my head I start planning what I can bring that will travel well. On the way home I stop at the grocery store and my plan takes shape.

The next morning we are up early. The director heads out to the set. The caterer heads to the kitchen. I intend to make a delicious, portable buffet. I construct focaccia sandwiches. I slice fruit for a salad. I chill sodas. I bake brownies. Now, how will I serve all this? I pull out baskets for the chips and trays for the sandwiches and brownies. I fill a big bowl with the fruit. I pack pickles, carrots, and olives. I remember the mustards and mayo. I load a big tub with bags of ice and put in the cans of soda and bottles of water. Don't forget the plates, napkins, and silverware! Ready.

At 11 o'clock I load everything in the car and head out to the set. Since I don't want the sound of my car pulling up to ruin a shot, I park and walk over the last hill to see how things are going.

"We'll be ready for lunch after this next shot. You can pull up and get things set up in the tent."

I unpack the coolers and set up the lunch trays. It's a simple spread, but everyone appreciates the homemade eats. Warm brownies will make just about anyone happy.

So for all the weekends of production, I became the caterer. I plan with care to keep them happy. I never serve the same thing twice. The only pay these folks will get is the experience of practicing their craft and the food I provide. My pleasure. I received my one—and-probably-only-ever—screen credit: *Catering—Lisa Bogart*

Sometimes it's not obvious what you should do. Sometimes you are set to be an observer and then thrust suddenly into action. Keep watch, you may be in the right place at the right time. So be ready to recognize how to use your gifts of hospitality.

Dear Father, Show me the ways to use my gifts when opportunities fall in my lap. Give me courage when I find myself in the right place at the right time. Help me to act on my good intensions. Amen.

Food for Thought

- When did you find yourself in the right place at the right time? Did you act on your impulse to show hospitality?

• Act on your good intensions.

Focaccia Sandwich

1 focaccia bread (flatbread from the deli)
8 slices prosciutto
½ cup mozzarella cheese
1 cup arugula, trimmed
1 Tbsp. sun-dried tomatoes
2 tsp. balsamic vinegar
Fresh ground pepper to taste

Carefully slice the focaccia bread in half, making two thin pieces. Place side-by-side on a work surface. Assemble sandwich starting with prosciutto, then cheese, arugula, and sun-dried tomatoes. Drizzle with vinegar and sprinkle with pepper. Cover with the other side of the focaccia bread. Cut the sandwich into four quarters. Wrap each piece tightly in foil. Bake at 300° for 15 minutes.

Do Something!

When I came out of the grocery store, the sun was just starting to set. The gray storm clouds from an hour ago were now brilliant orange. I stared at the sky knowing the next half hour was going to be beautiful. With three flavors of ice cream melting in the trunk, I drove off to a favorite walking spot. I ran down the muddy trail to the first clearing and stood still watching. It had rained for an entire week. Now a spectacular sunset splashed out in all its quiet glory. I had rushed to see it, craved the fleeting colors, strained to see every nuance.

As I walked back to my car I wondered about my drop-everything desire to see a terrific sunset. Do I have that kind of joy about other displays of God's glory? Do I run to church on Sunday morning eager to worship? Do I hunger to study God's Word? Do I look for ways to use my gift of hospitality? I rush off to see the obvious, but I often overlook the everyday. I don't want my road to be paved with good intentions. I want to act on the impulses to create hospitality with as much enthusiasm as I brought to chasing down a fleeting sunset.

I want to obey the impulse to act on an idea in the heat of an enthusiastic moment when it carries the most conviction rather than waiting for the watered down version zapped of all energy. Drop everything to enjoy a sunset. Drop everything to make room for tea with a friend.

It's exciting to read about all kinds of hospitality ideas, and we have every intention of trying out some of those good ideas. It was fun to read and it sounded good at the time, but acting on this will take a little effort. Don't let your road be paved with good intentions. Do something!

Food for Thought

- Do you stifle your impulses to use the gift of hospitality? How?

- What is nudging you? Is it time to act on those good intentions?

To replace the ice cream flavors melting in my trunk, try this homemade family favorite:

Mickelson Caramel/Vanilla Ice Cream
3 cans Eagle Brand sweetened condensed milk
3 pints half and half
3 half pints of cream
4 Tbsp. vanilla

Caramelize the sweetened condensed milk: Place the cans, unopened, in a large pot. Cover the cans with water, so they are submerged with a half inch of water on top. Bring the water to a boil. Reduce heat and simmer the cans for 3 hours. Fill with more water as necessary. Let the cans cool to room temperature and then chill them for several hours.

Put the caramelized milk in a large bowl and add the cream in small amounts to avoid lumps. Then add the half and half and vanilla. Place the mixture in ice cream maker and follow instructions for the machine. We used to make this in a hand crank model, so the next step would be several hours of turning.

I'm Glad You Could Come

I'm so glad we had this time together,
Just to have a laugh or sing a song.
Seems we just get started and before you know it,
Comes the time we have to say so long.

Carol Burnett ended her variety show with this little song every week. I thought of this while I was considering how to tell you good-bye. I'm so glad you came in for a visit. It sums up just how I feel. I hope you found some new insights into the wonderful gift of hospitality. And I trust you had some fun along the way. Hospitality is a present from God to you, unwrap it soon and share it with as many guests as you can. It's a gift with a lifetime guarantee.

Before you go, don't forget your party favor—another recipe I love to make and eat. It didn't fit in the book anywhere else, but I want to share it with you, so it's the perfect parting gift. See what you think. Maybe it will fit into your party plans. Or maybe it's time to treat your family to something new.

Cinnamon Pull-Apart Bread
    3 tubes (10 pieces each) buttermilk biscuits
    1 cup sugar
    3 Tbsp. cinnamon

½ cup butter (DO NOT use margarine)
1 tsp. vanilla
Nonstick cooking spray

Spray a bundt pan with nonstick cooking spray and set aside. Open all the biscuit packs and cut each piece in half so you have a total of 60 pieces. In a large Ziploc bag combine the sugar and cinnamon. Place approximately 10 pieces in the bag at a time and coat with the mixture. Repeat till all the pieces are covered. After coating pieces, place them evenly in prepared bundt pan. In a small saucepan melt the butter and then add vanilla. Remove from heat. Stir in the left over cinnamon sugar mixture and mix well. Pour this evenly over the pieces in the bundt pan. Bake at 350° for 35 minutes. Remove from oven and let cool about 5 minutes then flip onto a serving plate.

Finally, I invite you to visit my Web site: LisaBogart.com anytime for a weekly devotional, hospitality insights, and other fun things.

Enjoy!

Lisa

Recipe Index

Almonds
    Spicy Almonds 27
Artichokes
    Warm Artichoke
        Dip 153
Biscotti
    Minichip 149
Brownies
    Malted Glazed
        Brownies 78
Cakes
    Carrot Cupcakes 112
    Chocolate Pound
        Cake 82
    Spice Cake 142
Caramel
    Mickelson Caramel/
        Vanilla Ice
        Cream 182
Carrot Cupcakes 112
Cheese
    Iron Sandwich 113
Chex Mix 147
Chocolate
    Biscotti with
        Minichips 149
    Chocolate Pound
        Cake 82
    Confetti Cookies 22
    Fudge, Whit's 130
    Dirty Dessert in a Dixie
        Cup 112
    Malted Glazed
        Brownies 78
Cinnamon Pull-Apart
    Bread 183
Cookies
    Confetti Cookies 22
    Gingersnaps 132

Sugar Cookies,
    Mickelson 138
Deviled Eggs 76
Dirty Dessert in a
    Dixie Cup 112
Eggs Benedict with Easy
    Hollandaise 117
Emma's Gingersnaps 132
Focaccia Sandwich 180
Fruit Kabobs 113
Fudge, Whit's 130
Garlic Savories 77
Gingersnaps, Emma's 132
Grammy Mabel's Sweet
    Rice 135
Hamloaf 127
Hollandaise Sauce 117
Ice Cream
    Mickelson Caramel/
        Vanilla Ice
        Cream 182
Iron Sandwich 113
12 Layer Jell-O Salad 124
Kabobs (fruit) 113
Mickelson Caramel/Vanilla
    Ice Cream 182
Mickelson Sugar
    Cookies 138
Molasses
    Emma's
        Gingersnaps 132
Muffins
    Orange Muffins
        158
Orange Muffins 158
Patient Pork Ribs 167
Pecans, Vanilla 27

Pudding
   Grammy Mabel's Sweet
      Rice   135
Prosciutto
   Focaccia Sandwich 180
Ribs
   Patient Pork Ribs   167
Rice
   Grammy Mabel's Sweet
      Rice   135
Sandwiches
   Focaccia Sandwich 180

Iron Sandwich   113
   Pocket Sandwich   155
Sausage
   Pocket Sandwich   155
Spicy Almonds   27
Spice Cake   142
Vanilla Pecans   27
Warm Artichoke Dip   153
Whit's Fudge   130

Alphabetized Recipe List:

12 Layer Jello Salad   124
Biscotti with Minichips   149
Carrot Cupcakes   112
Chex Mix   147
Chocolate Pound Cake   82
Cinnamon Pull-Apart
   Bread   183
Confetti Cookies   22
Deviled Eggs   76
Dirty Dessert in a
   Dixie Cup   112
Eggs Benedict with Easy
   Hollandaise   117
Emma's Gingersnaps   132
Focaccia Sandwich   180
Garlic Savories   77
Grammy Mabel's
   Sweet Rice   135

Hamloaf   127
Iron Sandwich   113
Kabobs (fruit)   113
Malted Glazed Brownies 78
Mickelson Caramel/Vanilla
   Ice Cream   182
Mickelson Sugar
   Cookies   138
Orange Muffins   158
Patient Pork Ribs   167
Pocket Sandwich   155
Spice Cake   142
Spicy Almonds   27
Vanilla Pecans   27
Warm Artichoke Dip   153
Whit's Fudge   130

Web Sites and Other Resources

You may have laughed at the story of my mom leaving her comfort zone and venturing into cyberspace. The truth is, I am not far behind her. I may be comfortable tapping away on the computer, but I am not so keen on the Web. I just don't think that way. I don't use a computer much in my job. At home I have e-mail but not a cell phone. I like technology but only to a point. I still feel intimidated when faced with a new program to learn or device to figure out.

I tease my husband that I married him for tech support. Rod can troubleshoot anything I need, hardware to software. And if he's not home, my son comes to my rescue. I did not grow up with computers as Zach has; he knows no fear. He clicks and surfs. I remember learning to use a Macintosh. I got very frustrated with key commands because I didn't know you could hold two keys at once. Shift Apple D. Oh, you hold all those keys at once? You know on a typewriter that jams the keys. See, I'm old-fashioned.

So for my book to have a Web site section is

remarkable to me. I wanted to put in these notes for the Web-shy hostess. I know how you feel. You realize you can find any written information you might want on the Internet, audio and video as well, but finding it is perplexing. You have to think like a detective.

My husband is good at finding the information he needs. So I often cheat and ask him to help me. But I'm a big girl and should know how to do this. I don't want him to help me locate tea party cookie recipes. While researching this book I wanted to find a photographer I had read about. I couldn't remember the man's name, but I knew he took pictures of people around the world surrounded by a week's worth of groceries. Rod's advice was simple: Type in what you know. Are you kidding me? Okay, so I typed in: photograph week's worth of food. And I found what I was looking for! It was not the first item on the list but Google came through on item number 3. (By the way, the photographer's name was Peter Menzel, you can find him at menzelphoto.com) Search with what you know. Start with clues of things you want to find.

The next lesson in my Internet education from my husband was a change of perspective. "You found that on the Web? I'm surprised." was usually my response when Rod came up with the right information he needed. "I think you should change your question. You should not be thinking it was a surprise I found something, you should say, "I'm surprised you can't find it. It's all there." And he does mean all. You name it, you can find it.

So think like a detective. Type in what you know. Learn to look around without fear. Tread carefully though, because absolutely everything is there and you may indeed find things you'd rather not. (Spelling counts now.) However, with practice you will find what you need. I did. I've included the Web sites I used when writing this book. These sites were up and active in the fall of 2006. Things are constantly updated on the Internet. You may have to look around a little as sites change. You will find much more if you go nosing around. Be brave; you've come this far. Go for it!

Websites and Resources by Chapter

Chapter 1: Cleaning House
Flylady.com: organizational & cleaning tips
The Cure for the Common Life by Max Lucado: using your talents

Chapter 2: Excuses, Excuses
Too Much Stuff by Kathryn Porter
VikingCookingSchool.com: cooking classes

Chapter 3: Come On In

Evite.com: e-mail invitations

Searching for Bobby Fisher movie

Clipart.com: art to use for creating your own invitations

Dauphinepress.com: custom letterpress printed invitations

Mapquest.com: giving directions to the party

Google.com: giving directions to the party

entertaining.about.com/cs/dinnerparties/a/potluck parties.htm: hosting a potluck

cosmicwimpout.com: dice game

us.penguingroup.com: search mad libs

Apples to Apples, Pictionary, Outburst, Trivial Pursuit, Scrabble: games

Chapter 4: Let's Party!

Serendipity3.com: frozen hot chocolate

Frontiersoups.com: mail order soup mixes

soyouwanna.com/site/syws/hightea/hightea.html: How to host a High Tea

book-clubs-resource.com: information about book clubs

entertaining.about.com/cs/dinnerparties/a/dinner clug.htm: dinner club ideas

everydaytraditions.com/Traditions/Kitchen/Dinner Clubs: simple family rituals for connection and comfort (dinner club ideas and more)

netflix.com: DVD movies delivered to your home

Chapter 5: The Littlest Hostess

Kitchen for Kids: 100 Amazing Recipes Your Children Can Really Make by Jennifer Lowe

Kids in the Kitchen: 100 Delicious, Fun & Healthy Recipes to Cook & Bake by Micah Pulleyn and Sarah Bracken

Chapter 6: Grandma Know-How

Did you really expect grandma to be on the Internet? You can certainly find some old-fashioned yummy recipes though.

Chapter 7: Beyond Your Backyard

Once Upon a town, the Miracle of the North Platte Canteen By Bob Greene

GreatAmericanBakeSale.org: charity for hunger relief

Strength.org: stable communities that have enough to eat

CouponMom.com: coupons and ideas for supporting world hunger relief

Chapter 8: Thanks for Coming

LisaBogart.com: weekly devotional

More Helpful Web Sites and Resources

Cooking Light: magazine of recipes and food tips

Sunset: magazine of home, travel, food, and garden

House Rules, The Stylish Guide to Running a Home and Having a Life, by Clare Coulson

WeightWatchers.com: recipe of the day

List of Daily Devotionals

Upper Room: Upperroom.org

Our Daily Bread: rbc.org/odb/odb.shtmlchristthe savior.org/Default.aspx?tabid=186: A collection of many devotional sites

Christophers.org: nonprofit organization uses print, broadcast, and electronic media to spread a message of hope.

Good Reads About Hospitality

Hidden Kitchens: Stories, Recipes, and More from NPR's The Kitchen Sisters by Nikki Silva and Davia Nelson

Cooking for Mr. Latte by Amanda Hesser
Tender at the Bone by Ruth Reichl
Friendship Cake, A Novel by Lynne Hinton